HAUNTED
HIGH WYCOMBE

CW00969799

HAUNTED
HIGH WYCOMBE

Eddie Brazil

The
History
Press

This book is dedicated to the memory of my parents.

First published 2013

The History Press
The Mill, Brimscombe Port
Stroud, Gloucestershire, GL5 2QG
www.thehistorypress.co.uk

© Eddie Brazil, 2013

The right of Eddie Brazil to be identified as the Author
of this work has been asserted in accordance with the
Copyright, Designs and Patents Act 1988.

All rights reserved. No part of this book may be reprinted
or reproduced or utilised in any form or by any electronic,
mechanical or other means, now known or hereafter invented,
including photocopying and recording, or in any information
storage or retrieval system, without the permission in writing
from the Publishers.

British Library Cataloguing in Publication Data.
A catalogue record for this book is available from the British Library.

ISBN 978 0 7524 9145 5

Typesetting and origination by The History Press
Printed in Great Britain

CONTENTS

ACKNOWLEDGEMENTS

No book is ever written completely alone. I would like to thank those people who have helped with information and support during the writing of *Haunted High Wycombe*. Donna Barnett, Sally Scagell, Josie Atkins, Jan and Andy Maclean, Kate Osbourne, Michael Powell, my good friend and colleague Paul Adams, Peter Underwood, for his inspiration and kindness, Janet Kaye, and Matilda Richards at The History Press. And finally, to my wife Sue and my daughter Rebecca – my islands in the stormy sea.

INTRODUCTION

THE origins of this book go back almost fifty years, to the late spring of 1966, when, aged ten, I was living with my family in an eighteenth-century house in the Stockwell district of South London. We had moved into the house in November 1963, and as far as I was concerned the following two and a half years were an uneventful period of normal, family routines. However, on an ordinary June afternoon, a year before the hippy summer of love, that was all to change.

I had returned early from school around 4 p.m. to find no one at home. Letting myself in, I went and sat in the kitchen and read comics whilst I awaited the return of my grandmother. It was unusual for the house to be empty during the afternoon, as my Gran was normally at home and my father, who was a shift worker, would either be asleep or getting ready to go to work.

As I sat in the kitchen I became aware that the house had become unnaturally still and quite. The muffled sounds of the traffic and the shrieks and shouts of children playing outside seemed to have been silenced, and once or twice I looked up from my comic to peer quizzically around the quiet room.

Without warning, my younger brother's toy robot, which he often left wherever he last played with it, clicked and whirred into life and began marching across the floor towards me. The sudden breaking of the silence jolted me from my chair, and I got up, went over and stopped the robot. There was no indication as to why it had inexplicably burst into movement. I put it back in its box and returned to my seat with a puzzled frown.

It was sometime later that I suddenly heard a door upstairs close with a sharp slam, followed by footsteps.

The author's boyhood home in Stockwell, South London, where he first experienced the paranormal.

My immediate thought was that one of my brothers, or my father, was at home and now coming downstairs. And yet the sound of the descending footfalls on the stairs, and the way they seemed to edge tentatively down each step, made me listen up. It didn't sound like my father's measured tread, or the rushing eagerness of one of my brothers. At once the thought came to me that it might be an intruder who had broken into the house and, on hearing my return, was now cautiously coming down the stairs to make their escape. The footsteps reached the bottom floor and seemed to halt outside the kitchen. I sat transfixed, my eyes on the door, heart thumping, waiting to see who would enter.

I was certain that if I got up and opened the door I would be confronted by a large man with a stocking over his head and a crowbar in his hands. Yet, I didn't need to, for noiselessly and without warning, the door swung open on its own. I quickly sat upright, half expecting someone to enter, but no one did. I eventually mustered enough courage to get up and go and look out into the hall. It was then that I realised that the sounds were not those of one of my family or the clumsy footsteps of a burglar. The hall and the stairs were empty. I immediately panicked and bolted from the kitchen and into the garden, too frightened to re-enter the house.

The arrival of my grandmother soon after restored an air of normality to the situation, and I went back inside, although not without some trepidation. My cautious looks around the room, out in the hall and up the stairs brought from her a knowing look that seemed to say, ah, so you have heard it too? Indeed, my grandmother and my father had both experienced odd incidents in the house. I was to later learn that such was my parents' concern that my brothers and I would become so frightened if we became aware of what was occurring that both of them would try to ignore it. On certain days, when alone in the house, my grandmother would hear footsteps in empty rooms and doors closing by themselves. During the night, my father would often hear the front door of the house open and close, followed by footsteps that came along the hall and ascended the stairs. The footsteps would pause outside his bedroom before continuing up to the top floor. Getting out of bed, he would open the door and emerge out onto the cold, dark landing to see if there was anything out of place, and check that we were all in our rooms asleep, which we were. Eventually we moved from the house without discovering a reason for the strange disturbances.

One might have thought that my experience of living in a haunted house, and the encounter with disembodied footsteps and doors opening of their own accord, would have made me wary of the paranormal, or anything that went bump in the night. Yet, on the contrary, it awakened in me a fascination with the supernatural and ghosts, which has continued to this day. It is a road that has led to a collaboration with veteran British ghost hunter Peter Underwood and my close friend and colleague, paranormal historian Paul Adams, and the writing of *The Borley Rectory Companion: The Complete Guide to 'The Most Haunted House in England'* (The History Press, 2009), countless visits to alleged haunted sites, a study of haunted churches and, ultimately, to the book you are now reading.

Yet, it was also whilst living in Stockwell that I glimpsed hints of a future direction in my life. Each evening, as I played outside my front door, I would notice a single-decker Green Line bus which trundled along the road. Emblazoned across its destination panel were the words 'High Wycombe'. I wonder where High Wycombe is, my inquisitive young mind would think. The name, at least to a youngster growing up in the grime and noise of the capital, seemed to have a bit more allure than the place names of my local area such as, Clapham, Balham, Brixton or Tooting. It conjured up visions of a lofty, rural idyll, with fields, farms, woods and meadows.

It would be twenty years later that I got my first look at High Wycombe when, on a weekend in 1985, my future wife Sue, a native of the town, introduced me to the district during a visit to see her family. Wycombe, at least its centre, I discovered, was not at all high, for it sits within a long valley of beech-covered slopes within the Chiltern Hills, thirty miles north-west of London. But appearances can be deceptive. The name is derived from the Wye Valley high above the river Thames. And it really is so; if you stand in the middle of the high street you are level with the dome of St Paul's Cathedral in London.

In AD 800, it was neither hamlet, village or town but 'Wicumun' – meaning the farm or settlement in the valley. Three hundred years later and it is recorded in the Domesday Book as having twenty-seven villagers and eight serfs. Hughenden, Bassetsbury and Crendon are all listed as distant hamlets. Today's heavily developed areas, such as Castlefield and Micklefield, were, as late as 1930, still areas of unspoilt, rolling countryside. By 2010, High Wycombe had become the largest town in Buckinghamshire, with a population of almost 170,000 people. Its centre is a mixture of old and new, and throughout the years the town has grown and expanded up and across its surrounding hills with housing and commerce, in particular the furniture industry which for many years Wycombe was justly famous for. Sadly, today, that industry has now almost disappeared within the town. Nonetheless, the lofty rural idyll I had imagined as a child can, happily, still be found in its surrounding countryside.

Like many towns throughout Britain, High Wycombe is not without its ghosts, many of which we will encounter throughout these pages. If the houses, churches, ancient inns, roads and streets of a town are the fingerprints of all who have left their mark, then its ghosts are the memories of its past. Neolithic wanderers, Bronze- and Iron-Age dwellers, Roman invaders, Saxon settlers, and Norman conquerors have all left traces of their occupation in what would become this unassuming Chiltern market town. It has been said that such past events and peoples can leave

echoes; reverberations of episodes and incidents now long forgotten, but which linger on into the present until someone, in the right time and place, catches a glimpse of that lost past. Are ghost sightings visions of what has gone before, or are they proof of an afterlife? The answers, or some of them, it is hoped, are to be found within this book.

Our exploration of Wycombe's haunted sites is divided into four chapters. The first looks at those phantoms and ghosts which have been encountered on the open road, in fields, woods and open spaces. The next takes a look at the town's ancient and modern haunted buildings. The ghosts of West Wycombe (the site of the infamous Hellfire Club) are examined in Chapter Three, whilst those readers who would like to continue their ghost hunting in the towns surrounding Wycombe are provided with a number of haunted sites in Chapter Four. Throughout the book, to illustrate that the ghosts encountered in Wycombe are not unique, I have included incidents of paranormal phenomena recorded across Britain that are similar to those strange episodes that have been reported in and around the town and district.

The subject of ghosts can be a controversial one; either you believe in them, or you don't. To the sceptic they are nonsense unworthy of a second thought, whilst to the believer they represent fundamental questions regarding the nature of human beings, our existence and the greatest mystery facing us all – what happens when we die? Yet, such weighty concerns should not reduce us to endless navel-gazing or furrowed brows. Ghost hunting is not only fascinating but fun too. In recent years, investigating the paranormal and conducting haunted house vigils has become something of a popular hobby, with numerous ghost-hunting clubs and groups being established throughout the country. On any given weekend, instead of going out to the theatre, pub or restaurant, many ghost-hunting enthusiasts will happily sit in the draughty, darkened rooms, corridors and cellars of alleged haunted houses waiting for something paranormal to happen or appear. Most of the time they will return home disappointed after experiencing nothing strange or mysterious. And this, rather frustratingly, is what 99 per cent of ghost hunts are like. Yet, there will be those occasions when a long, tiresome vigil at a haunted site will result in the intrepid observer being rewarded with a fleeting glimpse into the unknowable, but intriguing world of the supernatural.

But what of High Wycombe's ghosts? The reader may wonder what chances there are of encountering them. Who can tell? As we will discover throughout this exploration of the town's haunted heritage, we

have yet to fully understand how the paranormal works, and why ghosts appear when and where they choose, and how they can interact, mentally and physically with us. It has been said that successful ghost hunters need the investigative powers of a detective, the reasoning of a scientist and the patience of a saint, for he will need all three disciplines in his quest for the true nature of ghosts.

In 1997, a team of paranormal researchers decided to hold a lengthy vigil at Chingle Hall in Lancashire, reputedly the most haunted house in Britain, where it was said that anyone who entered its doors would not leave without having an experience involving a ghost. The team's investigation was to last a week, but by the sixth night, with nothing whatsoever of a paranormal nature occurring, the researchers came to the conclusion that the twelfth-century house was haunted by nothing more than rumour and exaggeration, and they decided to end the vigil. As one of the team was collecting his gear from an upstairs room, he heard soft footsteps outside. Looking into the corridor, he was astonished to see the figure of a cowled monk standing silently at the far end. The 'brother of mercy' had his head bowed and his arms clasped in front of his habit. The figure remained motionless for a few moments, before turning to the right and vanishing through a wall. You see, you never know when a ghost is going to show up.

I hope you enjoy reading this book as much as I have writing it. If you have had your own experiences with the paranormal, by all means please get in touch with me. They would be welcome additions to either a future edition of *Haunted High Wycombe*, or in a sequel volume. And lastly, what are my own views on ghosts, do I believe in them? I will leave it to the Bard of Stratford to answer: 'There are more things in Heaven and Earth, than are dreamt in your philosophy.'

Eddie Brazil, 2013

1

THE HAUNTED TOWN PART ONE

Roads, Highways and Woods

THE ghosts and phantoms which are alleged to haunt High Wycombe are many and varied, and they include a rich panoply of paranormal phenomena no lover of haunted houses or ghostly happenings could fail to be frightened or fascinated by. Throughout this exploration of the town's haunted heritage we will meet not only unearthly horsemen, phantom motorcars, headless spirits and ghostly children, but also spectral coaches, disembodied footsteps, 'black magic' ghosts and kind dog-loving monks.

However, before we embark on our journey into Wycombe's paranormal past, we should perhaps first ask what is a ghost, and why do places become haunted? How is it that certain houses, public buildings, open spaces, lonely lanes and highways become areas where strange and bizarre incidents occur? Incidents which would appear to be outside the realm

of the established laws of physics and science, giving those who are fortunate enough to witness it, a glimpse into the fleeting and unknowable world of the supernatural.

The most immediate and readily acceptable answer, certainly to a champion and supporter of ghostly phenomena, is that a ghost – the spirit of a dead person – has returned to haunt the place in which they lived, or the person they loved during life. Following death, until he or she can move on to a higher form of consciousness, which a religious person might call heaven, they are doomed to wander the earth, or in our case the streets and buildings of High Wycombe, searching for an unobtainable desire or unfulfilled need. As unsuspecting observers we will, if we are in the right place at the right time, witness incidents and manifestations which are as yet unexplainable to modern-day knowledge; those indistinct figures or shadows which we fleetingly catch out of the corner of our eye as we make our way home after dark through the silent town or countryside, or perhaps the strange and mysterious sounds which awaken us during the small hours.

Yet, there are as many theories to what ghosts are as there are ghosts. They include mental imprint manifestations, atmospheric photograph ghosts, crisis apparitions, ghosts of the living, stone tape visions and teenage-angst-induced poltergeists. If they all have one thing in common it is their rejection by established science as evidence of an afterlife, and that they are seen as preternatural phenomena which will eventually be proven, by scientific means, to have a rational explanation.

Whatever ghosts are, we know that they have been reported from around the world for thousands of years. The first recorded account of a poltergeist haunting, contained in the *Annales Fuldenses* chronicle, took place in Bingen, now in modern Germany, 800 years before the birth of Christ. In the first century, Greek historian Plutarch reported the haunting of a public bath in Rome. Fifty years later Roman scholar, Pliny the Younger, carried out what is considered to be the first serious investigation of a haunted house in Athens.

Yet, despite years of research carried out by paranormal investigators, notably the Society for Psychical Research, established in 1882 by a group of Cambridge academics, we are no nearer to fully comprehending those things that 'go bump in the night'.

Perhaps one theory which might account for the ghosts and phantoms that are said to haunt High Wycombe, and one which would probably find a place on the scientific table for discussion, is that of the stone tape. The term 'stone tape' first appeared in the early 1970s following the television play of the same name written by Nigel Neal. It speculates that inanimate materials such as the stone or brick walls of a building can absorb a form of energy released from living beings during moments of stress, or harrowing and traumatic episodes, such as tragedy or death. At a later date, a person possessing psychic or mediumistic abilities, on entering the building where the drama took place and acting somewhat like a psychic video player, will sense, hear or witness a recording of the event. According to this hypothesis, ghosts are not spirits of the dead but simply non-interactive recordings similar to a film or television picture.

Most modern-day parapsychologists look upon the stone tape theory as a possible explanation for ghosts, although the hypothesis is not a new one. Elenor Sidgwick, president of the Society for Psychical Research in 1908 and wife of one of its founding fathers, Henry Sidgwick, proposed the theory that objects such as furniture or buildings can absorb psychic energy or impressions which could, over time, be transmitted to people.

Perhaps the classic example of a stone tape vision occurred in the city of York in 1953. Eighteen-year-old apprentice plumber, Harry Martindale, was installing new pipework in the cellar of the Treasurer's House located within the grounds of York Minster. As he was knocking through a part of the cellar wall he heard the sound of a trumpet. At first he thought the sound was coming from a radio elsewhere in the building. Yet, as he listened, it seemed that the blare from the trumpet was emanating from the wall of the cellar. It gradually got louder until, much to the young man's shock and terror, he saw a man dressed in the garb of a Roman soldier walk out from the wall. Directly behind him emerged a white horse upon which sat a centurion who, in turn, was followed by a troop of Legionnaires who proceeded to march across the cellar floor and disappear through the far-side wall. As the soldiers moved across the room, Martindale said he could hear the clop of hooves on the cobbled floor and also the soft murmuring of voices, but with no discernible language. The terrified apprentice fell back off his ladder and scurried to a corner of the cellar shaking with fear. When the last soldier had vanished through the other side of the cellar wall, Martindale fled from the room.

It would seem that what Martindale witnessed on that day were not the spirits of dead Roman soldiers, but a psychic recording of a procedure that must have occurred on a daily basis in York, for the city, or to give it its Roman name *Eboracum*, was a garrison town with the continual coming and going of troops. The apprentice was to later learn that the floor of the cellar, which had become forgotten under centuries of development, once formed part of a road that entered York, and what he witnessed was a troop of Legionnaires returning to their barracks. Yet, what triggered the playback of the vision, and why Martindale was able to observe an incident which had occurred nearly two thousand years ago, remains a mystery. Perhaps the easiest explanation is to say that Martindale was the right person in the right place at the right time, for even though the vision of the Roman soldiers had been witnessed previously and subsequently by others, not all who had visited the cellars were fortunate to share his experience.

If a stone tape apparition requires the fabric of a building to hold the psychic data of the recording, what are we to make of those ghosts who have been reported appearing in the open, on our roads, woods and fields? Our first foray into Wycombe's haunted past begins with those spectres encountered late at night by those travelling along lonely roads.

You are just as likely to experience a ghost on the highways and byways which criss-cross and circumvent High Wycombe as you are in one of the towns many centuries-old half-timbered buildings. The most commonly reported apparitions seen on the road after dark are phantom pedestrians who, once viewed in the beam of the cars headlights, are nowhere to be seen in the rearview mirror once the vehicle has passed, or, rather more alarmingly, those figures who step out in front of a speeding car only to vanish at the point of impact. The panic-stricken driver, convinced he has run down a real person, hastily goes to tend to the injured individual only to find there is no one there and the road is deserted.

Phantom coaches are an ingrained part of British folklore. Almost every part of the country can claim to have its ghostly coach and pair rattling through the night, driven, so tradition demands, by a headless coachman, and pulled by snorting, black steeds galloping madly through the sleeping village. The Chiltern Hills are abound with such tales. Nonetheless, despite their romantic, ghostly associations, coaches, before the advent of the railways, were the only practical means of long-distance travel between cities, towns and villages. Even so, it could take almost a day to travel the 30 miles from London to Wycombe; only a little bit longer than today in Friday night rush hour traffic. The turnpike road system came to Wycombe in 1719 with the extension of the London to Oxford route, taking in Beaconsfield and Stokenchurch. The toll organization of the roads provided funds for their upkeep and maintenance. Nonetheless, accidents occurred, and passengers were not only injured, but some lost their lives.

On an unspecified date in the 1860s or '70s, a coach en route from London to Oxford stopped at Beaconsfield to take on a fresh team of horses. It was late and the driver was eager to make for High Wycombe before dark. The evening was misty and the coach, on leaving the town, was soon lost within the increasing murk. The road from Beaconsfield to Holtspur, at that time a remote farmstead, is fairly level. Beyond the farmstead the route begins a long, gradual descent to Loudwater, which allowed the driver to pick up speed, thundering the fresh horses down White Hill (the present A40). At the foot of the hill, by Wooburn Moor, the road makes a slight dip. As the coach came hurtling down into the impenetrable fog, the horses panicked and the driver lost control and sight of the road, crashing the vehicle into the icy waters of a local pond. All on board, including the horses, perished. It is said that on the anniversary of the tragedy the cries and screams of the doomed passengers and neighing horses can be heard echoing throughout the area.

A spectacular disaster, worthy of a classic traditional ghost story. Yet, we immediately have a problem with this typically anecdotal tale, and it is one we will encounter with other alleged paranormal accounts throughout this book; the question of authentication.

The majority of ghost stories are, by their very nature, anecdotal or third-hand in the telling. An account of a haunting or ghost is related in the pub over a late-night pint by a person who has only heard the story in passing, and who soon relates his own version, which in turn is embellished and developed until the origin and truth of

the episode is lost in years of Chinese whispers. Another problem is the lack of modern-day eyewitness accounts of the alleged phenomena, and this, together with scant information regarding the original incident, makes it extremely difficult for the paranormal researcher to uncover any concrete evidence to substantiate the event. Nonetheless, two apparitions that have been witnessed close to the scene of the alleged Wooburn Moor coach crash may well lend weight to the veracity of the tale.

On a misty winter's night in 1936 a lorry was travelling down White Hill towards Wycombe. As it reached Wooburn Moor a man dressed in a

Wooburn Moor in Loudwater, where the cries of doomed coach passengers are said to sound.

black coat suddenly stepped from the side of the road and into the path of the truck. It was too late to stop and the driver couldn't avoid hitting him. Both the driver and his friend watched in horror as they saw the figure go under the vehicle. Convinced they had struck the man, they hastened from their cab to lend assistance, but when they went to look for the body there was nothing to be found: the road was empty. Even so, the distraught men informed the local police who also found no trace of the man. Later, the officer who had attended the scene informed the shaken driver that other people had reported the same thing happening to them on that stretch of road. Could the apparition of the man dressed in black be the spirit of one of the ill-fated passengers from the doomed coach?

The second phantom that has been reported close to where the truck collided with the figure, and which may also be the ghost of one of the doomed coach passengers, is a woman dressed in black Victorian clothing. She has been seen waiting by the entrance gates to Burleighfield House, a nineteenth-century mansion which stands back amidst the trees adjacent to the present-day Dreams roundabout. In 1998, on four separate occasions, her ghost was observed looking pitifully towards the site of the coach crash, holding one hand to her face, as if she was in a flood of tears or trying to shield her eyes from observing something terrible. Witness statements all report that the figure appeared solid and life like, and, but for her odd clothing, would not merit a second look. After remaining motionless for some seconds staring along the road she gradually melts away. It is possible that the phantom woman in black who has been seen standing at the gates to Burleighfield may have nothing to do with the coach crash tragedy as her ghost has also been seen in the house itself.

Burghleighfield House, built in 1863, is a grand twenty-room mansion standing in extensive grounds, with gardens which back onto open farmland. It became an artistic hotbed from 1962 until 1970, when it was owned by renowned stained-glass designer Patrick Reyntiens and his wife, Anne Bruce. Reyntiens designed the glass for the great hall at Christ Church, Oxford and the baptistery at Coventry Cathedral, and, with his wife, founded an independent art school that attracted creative spirits from around the world. Sadly, by the closing years of the twentieth century the house had fallen into disrepair, with only a few of its rooms habitable. In 2005, work began to restore the building and convert it into offices. Once the main building work was complete, the attic space and former living quarters for staff during its Victorian heyday were utilised as the hub for its computer systems and telecom relays. Engineers were employed to install the wiring and work commenced without any problems. A few days into the task, however, things took a strange turn. After packing up for the day, the engineers would take stock of their progress and calculated that the work would be completed in two weeks. Next morning, upon their return to the house, however, they were to find all of the previous day's installations had been tampered with. Wires had been pulled out, switches broken and equipment found strewn across the floor. Understandably, the engineers were not only mystified by what they discovered, but also angry. It seemed that someone had entered the building at night and sabotaged the work. Yet the owners of the house and the caretaker informed the men that Burghleighfield had been secure for the night with no sign of a forced entry, or indeed no theft or vandalism of any other part of the building. Although flummoxed, the engineers resumed their work, reinstalling the damaged section and adding new wiring to the system. Yet once again on returning the next morning, they found that the previous day's work had been tampered with. This bizarre occurrence was repeated on several more occasions, and all who had witnessed it began to scratch their heads and inevitably asked the question, 'Is the house haunted?' It seemed preposterous – how could a ghost wreak havoc with the installation of modern-day technology? Yet the engineers were to learn of rumours and stories about a woman dressed in black who was said to haunt the gardens. In the sunshine of a summer's day it seemed to be a laughable explanation.

Things were to take a sinister turn a few days later, however, when one of the engineers was working alone at the top of the house. He was a newcomer

Burghleighfield House, said to be haunted by a mysterious woman in black.

to Burghleighfield and was unaware of the strange events that had been taking place. His colleagues were outside on the lawn taking a tea break when the man came rushing from the house in an agitated state. His first words to his fellow workers were, 'I am not bloody working up there on my own'. It seems he was preparing to finish off some installation work and join them for a break when he heard what sounded like sibilant whisperings emanating in the room. At first he thought it was a trick of sound and that the soft murmurings were coming from a room below. Yet, as he continued to work he had the uncomfortable feeling that someone was standing behind him. The feeling was so intense that more than once he quickly swung around expecting to see a person,

but the room was empty. What made him flee was slightly more disturbing, however. He was about to pack up and come down stairs when he felt the icy sensation of a cold hand being laid on his shoulder.

The shocked engineer was to later learn what had been occurring within the house and the stories of the woman in black. Yet, ghosts or no ghosts, the installation of the telecom relays had to be completed, and it was decided that the men would work together and late into the evening to get the job finished. It seemed to do the trick as no more strange incidents were reported, the work was completed on time and the engineers were happy to move on to another site.

The arrival of staff at Burghleighfield, and the rush and

hubbub of the office day, seem to have neutralised any further paranormal incidents for none were reported at this time. On a bright Sunday morning in September, however, a workman arrived to clean the windows. The house was locked and empty for the weekend, but the cleaner was able to work on the exterior. Placing his ladder up at one of the first floor rooms he commenced cleaning. The view through the glass looked into an office and out through the door to the landing. Without any warning he saw the figure of a woman dressed in black Victorian clothes descend the stairs, cross the landing and carry on down to the ground floor. She had a most frightful, deathly pallor to her face, and seemed not so much to walk as to glide. The shock of seeing the woman nearly made him lose his grip on the ladder and fall. He quickly descended and pondered what to do. Even in the bright morning, with the reassuring sound of the nearby traffic, he felt disinclined to resume his work fearing what he might see through one of the windows. Letting his nerves and imagination get the better of him, he packed up and went home. The next day he returned and informed the gardener of what he had seen. The groundsman was not surprised to hear of his encounter, and told the cleaner of the tampering of the wiring in the upper rooms and that the house was said to be haunted. Who the woman in black is remains a mystery, but it would seem that one

The entrance to Burghleighfield House where the figure of a phantom woman in black has been seen.

of Burghleighfield's past occupants resents her former home being used in such a way and is prepared to let the present residents know her feelings.

Together with the sightings of the figure in the road, and reports of the cries and screams on the anniversary of the coach disaster, the spectre of the woman in black has not been observed for some years. Yet Burghleighfield house may well continue to be a site of paranormal activity. When the last of the staff have left at night and the house is shut up for the weekend, who can say what walks in the rooms and down the stairs? Is a house any less haunted if disembodied footsteps sound in the corridors and there is no one there to hear them? The laws and rules governing the supernatural, and why some hauntings ebb and flow at a particular site are unknown. Only time will tell if the woman in black chooses to once again manifest her presence.

There are many theories as to why some people see ghosts at a reputedly haunted site and others do not. We have already encountered the stone tape hypothesis, and the notion that human trauma can somehow be recorded into the fabric of a building and played back at certain times to a suitably 'tuned-in' person. Yet some parapsychologists would also expand the concept of the psychic recordings to include the very atmosphere of the site of the drama as also having the

facility to record and playback some form of psychic energy.

Pioneering maverick, parapsychologist and archaeologist, Thomas Lethbridge (1898–1971), who was keeper of Anglo-Saxon antiquities at Cambridge University, also came to this conclusion whilst walking with his wife on a beach near their home in Devon in the 1960s. It was a damp January afternoon, and as Lethbridge and his wife stepped on to the beach, both felt an overwhelming sense of gloom and fear descending over them like a blanket of fog. It became too much for Lethbridge's wife who, after only a short time, insisted they leave. She could sense something frightful.

The experience reminded Lethbridge of something he had encountered whilst walking with his mother in a wood near Wokingham when he was eighteen. It had been a lovely, yet humid, summer morning, when, quite suddenly, both of them experienced a horrible feeling of gloom and depression. They quickly hurried away from the scene, sensing that something was wrong with the place. A few days later, the body of a man who had committed suicide was found hidden by some bushes close to where they had been standing. After relating his experiences, Lethbridge discovered that others had also encountered similar unpleasant feelings at particular sites where some form of trauma had taken place. What intrigued him about the feelings of gloom and depression were the conditions in which they had been experienced. When Lethbridge and his wife came across the unpleasantness on the beach the weather had been damp. It was also damp and muggy when he and his mother had walked in the wood. Lethbridge theorised that a moist or wet atmosphere was in some way able to record negative emotions, which are basically electrical activities in the human brain, and be imprinted into their surroundings. It is known that underground water produces changes in the magnetic field and, significantly, magnetic fields are the means by which sound is recorded on tape with iron oxide. It is highly probable that the event which had caused Lethbridge and his wife to experience the feelings of gloom and depression on the beach, and the similar feelings he encountered walking in the wood, originally occurred on a damp wet day. It could also be argued that what he experienced can be described as a form of 'haunting', and if his psychic faculties had been more acute he would have seen a replay of the tragic event and probably an apparition of the man who had committed suicide. A person who was not at all tuned in would have experienced nothing untoward.

Interestingly, the coach crash at Wooburn Moor, and the subsequent reporting of apparitions connected with it, all took place in damp misty conditions. Yet whether or not this is the reason why phantoms have been reported at the site is unclear, for Lethbridge's theories on psychic tape recordings remain conjecture.

A few miles to the north of Wooburn Moor, across open country, is the village of Penn. It stands some 4 miles from the centre of Wycombe, and although the creeping fingers of urban ribbon development sneak ever closer, it still retains the feel of a Chiltern hill-top village. It is included in this survey as it contains no less than five ghosts; three of which may be considered traditional fireside tales. The remaining two, however, would seem to have far more in common with the disturbing terrors of a Hollywood horror movie.

The village is located between High Wycombe and Beaconsfield some 30 miles north-west of London, and the picturesque beech-covered hills and wooded valleys of the surrounding area belie its close proximity to the sprawling capital. The coming of the Beaconsfield railway in 1906 encouraged the construction of houses for commuters, which perhaps led poet laureate Sir John Betjeman to describe Penn as the 'Chelsea of the Chilterns'.

Penn Church, said to be haunted by a phantom horseman and a lady in white.

Indeed, the village has associations with many high-profile figures in British history, including eighteenth-century Parliamentarian Edmund Burke, composer Arthur Sullivan (of Gilbert and Sullivan), actor Stanley Holloway, the spy Donald MacLean, and David Blakeley, who was murdered by Ruth Ellis, the last woman to be hanged in Britain.

Perhaps the most prominent person linked with the village is Sir William Penn, founder of the city of Philadelphia, and after whom the state of Pennsylvania takes its name. He claimed Penn as his ancestral village, and his five sons and their families lie in the vaults beneath All Saints'

Church. However, Sir William, his wife and their children are buried in the churchyard at Jordans, 7 miles to the south east, where, so tradition says, the seventeenth-century Quaker meeting house was constructed out of timbers taken from the Mayflower. Despite the villages haunted reputation it seems that the Penn family do not feature in the paranormal activity reported there over the years.

In the eighteenth century, an unfortunate farmhand by the name of Clarke was killed when he was thrown from his horse, and for many years after it was his restless spirit which was said to bring terror to anyone who was passing through Penn after dark.

In 1880, four farmers, perhaps fortified by strong ale, decided to partake in a spot of ghost hunting. As they rode along the moonlit village lanes they suddenly saw the phantom rider as he appeared through a hedge and galloped off ahead of them. They set off in pursuit. The eerie thing was, however, that the horses hooves made no sound. When they reached Penn Church the apparition entered the churchyard whereupon it turned and laughed at the pursuers and vanished in a grey mist. The next day, the farmers returned to the spot where the ghostly rider had disappeared, and were alarmed to find that there were only four sets of hoof prints, not five.

Now, of course, this account has all the hallmarks of a traditional ghostly legend told endlessly around the Penn village fireside. But is it possible to prise some nugget of authenticity from such a typical anecdotal tale? Folk stories are rarely conjured out of thin air, and even the most outlandish have some grain of truth at their root. We can reasonably accept that at some period in the eighteenth century a farmhand by the name of Clarke was killed when he fell from his horse. Thereafter, the locals believed it was his restless spirit that haunted Penn churchyard and the village. What is curious is that the year 1880, over 100 years after the farmhand was killed, is singled out as a period when the ghost was particularly troublesome. Whether or not it was the restless spirit of Clarke we shall never know. Nonetheless, it could

The Crown Inn at Penn, where a woman in white is said to walk.

well be a case of folklore flesh being grafted onto the bones of an actual paranormal incident.

In the late 1980s, a figure in white was said to walk through Penn churchyard at night, passing through the east gate and descending Paul's Hill. The figure is described as a woman in pale flowing garments or wearing a white nightdress. When approached, the figure vanishes. The identity of the apparition is unknown, however, the village pub, the seventeenth-century Crown Inn which stands just across the road from the church, is also said to be haunted by an unknown woman in white. Could the spectre from the Crown also be the figure which walks in the churchyard?

The above stories of white ladies, phantom horsemen and doomed lovers no doubt belong to the romantic side of ghost tales which one could easily read to children at bedtime without causing too much alarm. Yet, the history of psychical research also contains countless accounts of paranormal incidents, as the two following examples will show, that defy explanation and which have been unnervingly disturbing for those who experience them.

The countryside around Penn is criss-crossed with many footpaths and bridleways which are popular with walkers. On a sultry, overcast day in August 1987, thirty-eight-year-old Sara Osbourne took her usual walk across the fields near Tylers Green. Her route began on a path which runs by the side of the Red Lion public house, down to a section which skirts Puttenham Place Farm, which at the time was derelict. Here, the paths fan out in different directions, but Sara continued on a circular route, which took her around by the edge of Pugh's Wood and back along to the north side of Puttenham Farm. The fields and footpaths were unusually empty of other walkers, and Sara recalls that the grey day seemed strangely still and silent. She had almost completed her walk and was nearing the farm when she looked ahead and saw a figure standing motionless on the path some hundred yards away. She stopped and became immediately aware that what she was seeing was not normal. The person appeared to be an extremely tall man dressed in a long black coat, which hung down below his knees. He wore what seemed to be white gloves, and his left hand hung by his side whilst his right, positioned at his midriff, pointed towards her. His whole attire seemed out of place and completely wrong for the sticky, humid day. However, as Sara stared at the strange figure she realised something that made her go cold and distinctly queasy. The head of the man seemed to be abnormally small as if it had been shrunk. Like the head of a baby implanted onto the neck of an adult. Yet there were no features – no eyes, nose or hair. It was just like

The path near Tylers Green, where Sara Osbourne encountered a frightful apparition.

a small stump protruding from the man's shoulders. The whole scene was disturbing, and made only more so as a distant rumble of thunder sounded across the darkening afternoon, and the first fat, splats of rain began to fall.

As the figure stood rigid and unmoving, seemingly staring at her, Sara began to feel threatened and scared. She wondered if the figure was some kind of optical illusion. The thought of continuing in the direction of the man and passing him was extremely distasteful to her. She turned and made her way back along the path, which led to the main road of the village. Before passing out of the fields and back into Tylers Green she looked back to see if the figure

had chosen to follow her. Much to her relief, and surprise, he was nowhere to be seen. However, even though the rain had now began to come down heavily, Sara's curiosity compelled her to retrace her steps part way back into the field to see if she could catch sight of the strange person. But there was no one there, and the whole area seemed empty of people.

Sara returned home unsettled and disturbed by the incident, and was at a complete loss as to an explanation. She did consider that the vision might have been the result of a hallucination, but she quickly dismissed this idea. The whole episode felt real and uncanny enough for her to flee the scene and, for weeks after, give her many sleepless nights. Following her strange encounter she refrained from taking her solitary walk across the fields, and it took some time for her to once again feel safe enough to so, and only in the company of friends.

The experience of Sara Osbourne is not only extraordinary and bizarre, but eerily creepy, and one wonders into what file such apparitions should be catalogued; ghosts, spectres, phantoms of the living, doppelgangers, evil spirits? Although hard to classify, such visions are not without precedent. In his book, *Ghosts over Britain*, Peter Moss describes the experience of Gladys Ewing from Aberdeen. In the early hours of New Years' Day, 1971, she was on her way to work at a local hospital near to her home. It was 5.30 a.m., and despite it being Hogmanay the streets were eerily empty. As she passed through a housing estate on her way to the bus stop she glanced casually in the direction she was going, and to her utter astonishment she saw an immense figure wearing a hood and a cloak standing on a patch of grass some hundred yards away. She was instantly paralysed by fear. All she could do was to stare uncomprehendingly at the gigantic, motionless figure that stood under the full glare of one of the street lamps. It seemed extremely tall, with the cloak reaching down to the ground, hiding legs and feet. The face wore a mask with two narrow eyes for slits, yet Gladys had no doubt that the figure was a real human being. Whether it was a reveller or an eccentric from the previous night, she did not know.

Without warning the figure raised one arm and began to beckon to her. Gladys felt compelled to move towards the figure, and with mounting terror she was inexorably drawn towards where it stood; when she was no more than twenty feet away from it, the form disappeared into the grass like a fading fog. Although Gladys' first impulse was to flee from the area, before she did so she stayed long enough to establish that there was nothing on the spot where the figure had vanished apart from unbroken and unmarked turf. Realising she had probably witnessed something paranormal she fled towards the bus stop and, hopefully, the company of other people.

These incidents seem to be random, isolated supernatural episodes which appear to have no reason or purpose, unless it is to alarm and frighten, which they certainly do. Significantly, each occurrence was never independently reported previously or subsequently, and for both Sara and Gladys it was their one and only encounter with the paranormal. We might label the incidents as psychical blips; supernatural abnormalities that remain apart from the main body of paranormal phenomena. Yet, that would seem to imply that psychic phenomena is bound by rules, and the episodes described are some kind of wayward paranormal anomaly, like a misbehaving child, which chooses to disobey the code. However, many supernormal encounters are of a similar nature, and although there are those that at first might appear to be nothing more than a chance meeting with something unnatural, there are others which have connections which may explain the phenomena.

On an October night in 1995, fifty-four-year-old Michael Powel went to Penn, eager to explore the adjacent fields with his metal detector for ancient artefacts such as coins, buttons and broaches dropped and lost over the centuries by long-gone residents of the village. However, past expeditions at other sites during the daytime had seen him flee the wrath of farmers outraged that their crops were being trampled and crushed by hooligan treasure hunters. Consequently, Powell decided to carry out his detecting activities under cover of darkness. Parking his car in a lay-by partway along Common Wood Lane, he made his way up through Pugh's Wood and out into the fields near to Puttenham Place Farm and onto the very path where Sara Osbourne had encountered the strange figure of the headless man eight years earlier. On this night, Powell would also come into contact with something equally uncanny and no less disturbing.

Listening for the bleep of his metal detector and keeping an eye out for vigilant landowners he silently explored the fields, yet after an hour of fruitless searching he decided that there was little, if anything, of worth to be unearthed. He decided to pack up and return home. He made his way back into Pugh's Wood and down to his car. He had only gone so far into the trees when he heard voices. He stopped and listened intently, and realised that they were the laughs and shouts of children. But he was puzzled; what were children doing in a wood at that hour? As he continued to listen, the voices seemed to be getting closer. It struck him that, even though it was 3 a.m., the children had to be accompanied by an adult, and if he was discovered he would be in the embarrassing situation of explaining his own presence at that hour. He remained still and continued to listen. He was relieved to hear the voices of the children heading away from him. Yet, just as he thought they had moved off to the far side of the wood, he once again heard them, but this time they were from his rear. He quickly spun around. The laughter and singing of the children were coming from behind him, and rapidly heading in his direction, but there was no sound of the snapping of twigs or the rustle of bushes, only the playful yelps and shouts of the youngsters. As the sounds came closer, Powell expected the children to appear, but there was nothing to be seen in the darkness of the wood. Just as quickly as the voices had sounded behind him they immediately changed course and now emanated from the direction of the fields, seemingly fading and then sounding close again. Powell swung left, right and behind, wondering what was happening. The sound of the children seemed to be all around him. It was at this point that he became scared and immediately realised that what he was hearing was abnormal. Hurriedly, he moved down through the wood and back to his car. He got in and, before starting the engine, wound the window down and listened. There were no sounds coming from the wood, only the wind in the trees. He quickly drove away shaking

his head, his eyes on the illuminated road, expecting at any moment to see two ghostly children walk out in front of him.

Michael Powell, who died in 2005, was a friend of the author of this book, and the above encounter was related over a pint in a Wycombe pub not long after the episode. Powell knew of my interest in ghosts and, convinced he had indeed heard the spirits of two children, asked if I could throw any light on his experience. At the time I couldn't. It appeared to be a one off incident, and one I had never before come across. If the phantom children had been experienced by others, then they had kept their silence. Powell never returned to the wood either

Pugh's Wood in Penn, where Michael Powell was terrified by the sound of phantom children.

by day or night, but for many years was intrigued and baffled by what he had heard that night. In his search for ancient relics, Powell had explored many locations during the small hours and often in places many of us would hesitate to venture after dark. But Powell took this all in his stride, and was not a person to become easily spooked by being alone in a field or wood at night. Yet his experience in Pugh's Wood had been the only time in his detecting career when he felt truly frightened.

The puzzle of the phantom children would have remained a mystery had a chance browse on the internet some years later not revealed a distressing yet intriguing coda to the story. On 19 November 1941, six-year-old Kathleen Trendle and eight-year-old Doreen Hearne were on their way home from Tylers Green School in Penn. They had reached the cross roads by Elm Road and Common Wood Lane, which runs alongside Pugh's Wood, when an army truck pulled up beside them. The driver leaned out of his cab and offered the two girls a ride. Both got in and the truck drove off in the direction of the village of Penn Street. The children did not return home that night, and three days later their bodies were discovered in a nearby wood. Both had been strangled and stabbed.

Close by were the tyre tracks of a lorry and a large patch of oil. There was also Doreen's gas-mask holder and a khaki handkerchief with the laundry mark, RA1019. A twelve-year-old boy had told police that he saw the two girls getting into the truck, and gave the unit identification marks of the lorry. The vehicle was quickly traced to 341 Battery, 86th Field Regiment, Royal Artillery, in Yoxford, Suffolk, and they soon came across the truck. The tyre tracks matched the impressions taken from the scene.

The driver was twenty-six-year-old gunner Harold Hill. He had the laundry mark and his fingerprints were found to match those on the discarded gas-mask container. When his kit was examined his spare uniform was found to have bloodstains on it. His plea of insanity was rejected and he was hanged at Oxford Castle on 1 May 1942.

It is tempting to connect Powell's experience in the wood with the murder of the two children, but, without further evidence, it would be hasty and flawed for the bodies of the two girls were discovered in Rough Wood, some way from where Powell had his encounter. It is possible that Powell was indeed aware of the murder of the two children, and had buried the knowledge of the tragedy deep within his subconscious. Being alone in a wood near to where the incident had taken place, and hearing unusual but natural nocturnal sounds, might well have triggered the belief that he was hearing the playful yelps of the

Amersham Road, where a faceless figure walks.

two phantom children. The fact that he was in woodland in the dead of night probably added to the aural illusion.

We move now from the fields around Penn back to the open road. In January 1971, Steve Bond and his wife were driving home to Wycombe along the A404, Amersham Road, when they had a strange experience. It was close to midnight as they were approaching the junction to Penn Bottom, Gravelly Way (B474), when they saw the figure of a man standing by the side of the road. The figure appeared so quickly that Steve had to swerve to avoid it. The night was clear but cold and the side of the road had wide grass verges but the figure seemed to come from nowhere.

For a couple of seconds the figure was lit up by the car headlights and Steve had a good view of it. He said that it was the figure of a stocky man wearing a sports jacket, with his head completely wrapped in bandages. Even more unusual was that the man had no face, just a sort of greyness. Steve drove on and said nothing for a while until eventually he asked his wife if she had seen anything odd back down the road, and she described exactly what her husband had seen.

A similar encounter was experienced by Mark Nursey and his girlfriend,

Four Ashes Road, where a green spectre has been encountered.

Allyson Bulpett, on the night of 20 September 1986, on Four Ashes Road which runs from Cryers Hill to Terriers about two miles outside of the centre of Wycombe. Located halfway along the road is a small cemetery, and local legend has it that the area is haunted by a giant faceless figure which appears within a grey mist.

It was close to midnight when the couple were nearing the cemetery and a large figure suddenly loomed into view. As the car approached they saw that it was a man completely dressed in green and standing nearly 2m tall. The figure began to wave at them, so Mark slowed his car,

whereupon the man stepped into the road, glared at them and then vanished. Mark described the figure as looking like it was wearing a big green jumper, but he couldn't make out its head or hands.

Mark and Allyson reported their encounter to a local newspaper, and a subsequent article describing their strange experience prompted others to come forward saying that they too had seen the green man. Most notable was a twenty-eight-year-old warehouseman, Phil Mullett, who had seen the figure in 1978 whilst driving along Four Ashes Road, within metres of where Mark Nursey and Allyson Bulpett had encountered it. It was 10.30 on a moonless night when the figure appeared from the right-hand side of the road. To avoid it, Phil drifted into the middle of the road whereupon the form turned towards him and waved its arms. It seemed that it was trying to warn him to keep back. Then it glided into the hedge on the other side of the road and suddenly reappeared, moved to the middle of the road, turned and lifted its arms. By then, Phil, even though he braked, could not avoid hitting it. Totally shaken, he got out of the car, convinced that he had run someone, or something, down. Yet, the road was deserted with no sign of the figure. He described the shape as about 2m tall and appearing perfectly solid. It was bright green, did not appear to have any hands or feet and, instead of a face there was just a misty grey round shape.

It remains a mystery as to what the three witnesses saw on Four Ashes Road. Some have suggested that it was the Green Man; a spirit of the forest which is associated with Pagan fertility rites. Although this would seem fanciful, Mark, Alyson and Phil remain convinced that they encountered a tall, green figure, which was there one moment and gone the next.

Night phantoms of the road are a far more common occurrence than one might expect, and have been witnessed over the years by many different people. Indeed, two members of the multi-million selling rock band Fleetwood Mac had their own strange encounter with a roadside apparition one night in 1965. Peter Green and Mick Fleetwood were then members of the little-known group, The Peter Bs, their leader being keyboardist Peter Bardens. Following an engagement at a club in Portsmouth, the band was returning to London in a van driven by the fourth group member, David Ambrose, by way of the A3. All four were seated in the front of the van as they were proceeding through Cobham at about 2.30 a.m. The night was clear with a few mist patches in some places along their route, and, as would be expected at that hour, the neon-lit streets were deserted. As the van rounded a bend a figure came into view on their side of the road. The group saw it simultaneously and realised it wasn't a normal person. The figure was walking along the pavement towards the van with his gaze fixed straight ahead. The group described the person as being abnormally tall, possibly over seven feet, wearing a long mackintosh which hung almost down to his ankles and it was radiating a kind of pale light. All observed that the face of the figure was that of an old man with a blank, expressionless stare, with eyes which were nothing but black sockets. His hands were down at his sides, and he seemed to be not so much as walking as gliding. As the van passed, two of the group members sitting nearest to the figure screamed in terror. The band were so unnerved at what they saw that they sped away from the scene immediately.

Their strange encounter later came to the attention of renowned parapsychologist, George Owen, who initially considered that the boys had experienced a collective telepathically relayed hallucination, possibly brought about through tiredness. He ultimately concluded that the group had probably observed a paranormal apparition. However, Owen's initial consideration of a hallucinatory vision may well provide a clue as to why some people do see strange anomalies whilst driving at night.

A paradox of the paranormal, despite what the presenters of the *Most Haunted* TV programme might have us believe, is that we rarely see ghosts when we are consciously looking for them. We experience the supernatural when we least expect to. Yet, if we do encounter an apparition, it would seem that certain conditions have to be in place. We have already looked at Lethbridge's psychic recording theory. But most psychic investigators would also agree that the mind has to be in a relaxed state, receptive and free from extraneous thoughts. Many ghost sightings are reported by people who have retired to bed for the night and are relaxed in that twilight world between sleep and wakefulness. They observe the apparition for a few

seconds, only to see it vanish when they have become fully aware of its presence. Similar conditions might be said to occur when driving at night.

We have all had the experience of driving home after a long and tiring day. The roads are empty, and we drive as if on auto-pilot as the mesmerising beam from the headlights illuminates the way ahead creating shadows and shapes along the roadside. Perhaps the radio is playing soft music at a low volume and the hum of the engine and the gentle movement of the car lulls the person into a relaxed state. As such, it might be said our consciousness becomes tuned to a different mode; one which may well be able to receive images and visions which are not only hallucinatory, in part, but also transmitted telepathically, and linked to the phenomena of crisis apparitions and phantasms of the living. It is only when we become fully aware of the apparition that our reverie is broken and the figure vanishes. Not all phantoms of the road, however, are witnessed during the hours of darkness.

One Sunday morning in 1987, eighteen-year-old Donna Barnett was driving up Abbey Barn Lane, which runs from Kings Mead Road to Flackwell Heath. It was a bright day, about 9 a.m., and she was looking

Abbey Barn Lane, where Donna Barnett came across a phantom car.

forward to spending some time with her boyfriend. As she went up the single-track road she saw a blue Fiat car coming towards her. At the wheel was a dark-haired man and beside him sat a fair-haired lady, both, as Donna reckoned, in their early twenties. The cars met and as she was very near to a passing place, Donna reversed back to let them pass. Once she had finished positioning her vehicle to let the other car through, she looked up and expected them to go past. But the car had vanished. This seemed impossible, for there was nowhere else for it to go. Donna would have certainly seen the Fiat go by. She looked in her mirrors and searched the road but there was no sign of the other vehicle. Shaken by the experience, Donna drove on to her boyfriend's house. She says she has no explanation of the event. The incident appeared to be totally real and even today she can still picture the young driver's face. It is unknown why or what Donna witnessed on that bright Sunday morning. The simplest explanation would be that she was mistaken and that the other car simply drove on and quickly went out of view. Yet she is adamant that this was not the case. One moment a blue Fiat car was there; the next it was gone.

Although this type of phenomena is baffling it is not without precedent. During the 1930s, a phantom red double-decker London bus on route number 7 was said to harass motorists at night in the North Kensington area. One motorist reported seeing the bus hurtling towards him down St Mark's Road. The lights on the top and bottom decks were on full, as were the headlights, but there was no sign of crew or passengers. The motorist quickly took action to avoid certain collision, but as he did so the bus suddenly vanished.

Phantom vehicles epitomise a problem for those who believe that ghosts are revenant spirits. If a ghost is the soul of a dead person returned to earth, how do we account for phantom cars, buses, horse-drawn coaches and other inanimate objects which act in a supernatural manner? Frustratingly for the paranormal investigator such incidents as that experienced by Donna Barnett only leave more questions than answers. As far as I can ascertain there

had been no previous or subsequent reports of sightings of the phantom Fiat, and it would seem that no amount of Sunday morning vigils at the spot in Abbey Barn Lane will reveal why a solid, nuts and bolts object can vanish into thin air. It is, as ghost-story writer M.R. James once observed, one of the rules of the paranormal which we have yet to understand.

The infrequency of ghost observations at a particular location after the initial sighting is also a problem for investigators, for it is difficult to substantiate the report or recognise any pattern to the phenomena and, of course, one never knows when a ghost is going to make an appearance.

Cock Lane, where two road ghosts have been seen.

One night in 1994 on Cock Lane, which is situated east of the centre of Wycombe, the figure of a woman in grey crossing the road was reported by a motorist as he drove along the lane in the direction of Tylers Green. When he drew close to the figure it suddenly vanished. What the driver saw is unknown, and following the encounter it would appear that there were no further sightings in the subsequent nineteen years. Nonetheless, back in the early 1980s another witness reported seeing the apparition floating towards him along the lane from the direction of Tylers Green. The terrified man fled, and when he looked back the ghost had vanished. Similarly, in Loakes Road in the centre of the town – and once home of Wycombe Wanderers football ground – the spectre of a woman in grey, riding a phantom horse has been witnessed galloping along the road up to the gates of Loakes House. Unlike the unknown ghost of Cock Lane, the phantom of Loakes Road is said to be that of a young girl who was killed when thrown from her horse in the eighteenth century. She is said to ride up to the house and vanish, but her horse makes no sound.

All are mysterious and beguiling incidents, and can technically be viewed as hauntings, yet, in each case we have a paucity of sightings. Two in just under twenty years at Cock Lane, and perhaps no more than a handful in two centuries in Loakes Road. In such circumstances it is possible that the episodes described can acquire their own tradition and have folklore flesh grafted onto bare paranormal bones ultimately obscuring the veracity of the original event. An example of this is the alleged haunting of Sandage Wood.

The wood, just to the south-west of High Wycombe, near the village of Lane End and right beside the M40 motorway, is said to be haunted by a ghost known as the Spangled Lady. Clad in jewellery, which sparkles in the moonlight, she is said to walk up to a gate at the end of the wood, where she stops. Standing there for a while, she looks out across the fields. When whoever it is she is waiting for fails to arrive she turns and retraces her path back into the woods. A typical romantic ghost tale, but for the psychic investigator one that is almost impossible to substantiate. With practically no recent first-hand reports of the phantom, we may ask how we know that the Spangled Lady waits at the moonlit gate for her unknown friend, for how many of us are in the habit of walking alone in a darkened wood at night to witness such phenomena? It is possible that the ghost of Sandage Wood has its origin in some kind of past paranormal incident, yet the passage of years has all but eroded the true facts of the story.

A similar ghost account that would seem to have its origin in a romantic tale of lost love is that of the lady in red who is said to haunt Wheeler End Common, which is situated some 8 miles west of High Wycombe. Her name was Anna and, in 1766, she had planned to wed her sweetheart. Tragically, ten days before the wedding, she died of a fever. Thereafter her apparition was said to walk the paths and lanes near the inn on Wheeler End Common where she had worked as a barmaid. In life she was fond of the colour red and always wore it. Those who saw the ghost reported that it was a young woman attired in a red dress. Her appearances were quite frequent in the nineteenth century, but thereafter sightings of the phantom became fewer.

In 1943, a girl walking across a field near to Wheeler End saw someone in a red dress. The day was bitterly cold, and the figure in red seemed to have no coat. It was snowing and the whiteness of the landscape made the ruby of the woman's clothes stand out. But before it could be ascertained who the solitary person in red was, she faded from view. Appearances of the lady in red continued into the 1940s, but the last reported sighting was in 1960.

The village of Flackwell Heath, which lies just a few miles south-east of the centre of Wycombe, has three ghosts that would also seem to have their origins cloaked in the mists of time. Many centuries ago a heretic by the name of Thomas Chase was incarcerated in a cell in Wooburn, where he suffered miserably for his beliefs. He was eventually murdered by his captors and his body buried, so it is believed, at the crossroads of Whitepit Lane and Juniper Lane. The Bishop of Wooburn, keen to avoid any responsibility for Thomas Chase's murder, declared that Thomas had committed suicide whilst in prison. It is said that his ghost roams the crossroads to tell you that he would never have taken his own life but was murdered.

Not far from the haunted crossroads is Treadaway Hill, where a phantom sister of mercy is said to walk with a candle cupped within her hands. It is believed that the unfortunate novice became lost, and in the darkness drowned in the River Wye.

The third of our Flackwell ghosts has even had an area and a poem celebrated in its honour. The Spirit of Spirit's Field tries to stop you from walking along a footpath that once crossed the fields here. It was a shortcut which took you through Fennels Wood, and then over the fields to Wycombe Marsh.

This land which once was 'Grubbins',
Where the Fifties houses stand,
Was also known as 'Spirit's Field'
And this was haunted land.
A footpath took you to the Marsh
Through deep, dark, Fennels Wood
And here a spirit barred your way
And scared you if it could.
Perhaps it was a helpful ghost
Who knew a safer walk
And tried to help you for the best
Although it couldn't talk.

(Poem by Sally Scagell)

It is not only phantom cars, coaches, white ladies and unearthly nuns that have been reported walking the highways of Wycombe. The sounds of ghostly armies marching to battle have also been heard tramping the lanes and fields of the Chilterns. Although some accounts of this type of phenomena are very much of an anecdotal nature, we shouldn't be too eager to dismiss them. If one accepts T.C. Lethbridge's theory of human trauma and emotions being recorded into the atmosphere of a site where tragedy and distress have occurred, it isn't surprising if the torment and anguish of men marching to battle leaves a trace of their bloody fate.

The opening battle of the English Civil War took place at Edge Hill in Warwickshire in 1642. Both Roundheads and Cavaliers fought to a brutal stalemate as thousands of men lay dead on the field. Some weeks later, when farmers returned to the battlefield to tend their herds, they reported that they could see and hear the two armies once more fighting in the sky above Edge Hill. So intrigued was King Charles I of the account of the spectral battle that he sent commissioners from London to examine the claims. They returned to the King and reported that they too had seen and heard the ghosts of Royalist and Parliamentarian soldiers fighting above the battlefield.

The marching of phantom armies aside, Wycombe cannot boast a re-enactment of a ghostly battle. During the Civil War, however, the town, being a Parliamentarian garrison, was twice attacked by the Royalists. In December 1642, a Royalist army marched from Oxford towards Wycombe, and skirted north of the town, advancing down Hammersley Lane and on to the Rye by way of Back Lane and Bassetsbury. The townsfolk were not slow in responding to the assault, and barricades were set up in Horsenden Lane (today's Queen Victoria Road). The Parliamentarian commander of Wycombe, Captain Haynes, managed to muster some 4,000 pike men, and fierce fighting commenced. During four hours of battle, the Cavaliers were pushed back on to the Rye, and their commander, Lord Wentworth, being wounded, fled the field. The fighting continued as the

Royalists retreated back across the hills north of the town towards Hazlemere, where it is believed a last-ditch skirmish was fought on what is now the golf club. Over a thousand men were killed, but Wycombe was prevented from falling into Royalist hands.

It is a frustration and fascination of psychical research that we still don't understand why certain paranormal phenomenon occurs. Why is it that the sounds of phantom armies have been heard marching along the lanes around Wycombe, and not the actions of a battle itself? The bloodiest battle of the English Civil War took place at Marston Moor in Yorkshire in July 1644. Thousands were killed, and one might have thought that such a bloody clash would indeed leave a psychic trace of the conflict. Yet, it is only the solitary ghosts of individual soldiers, standing forlornly on the battlefield, that have been witnessed over the years.

As paranormal historian Paul Adams has observed, ghost hunting is very much a discipline of phenomenology, which is the study and classification of related paranormal phenomena. All researchers can do is collect information regarding paranormal experiences as accurately and truthfully as possible, try to sift the folklore from the truth and try to gain an idea of what is going on. Nonetheless, there are other accounts of ghosts experienced throughout Wycombe which would seem to hold water far better than those tales obscured by lack of evidence or romantic embroidery.

The Irish Club stands tucked away in Station Road, which is situated a little to the east of Wycombe's main centre. The building, parts of which date back to the eighteenth century, has been the focus for the town's Irish community for the past forty-three years. As well as providing a meeting place for the Emerald Isle's ex-patriots, it also serves as a venue for parties, receptions and social gatherings; the author has himself attended a few 'get togethers' there. The paranormal incident that concerns us here relates not to the club but a site adjacent to it, although it is possible that the apparition observed might be linked in some way to the building.

One Saturday night in 2006, eighteen-year-old Stephen Wagner attended a party at the club. The evening's festivities turned out to be a pretty boring and average event and soon he took himself outside to get a bit of fresh air. Outside the club there is a small park area, not much more than a square patch of grass with a few trees and a bench. As Stephen waited, he looked over to the bench and, in the faint glow of the street lamps, saw the figure of a man appear seemingly out of thin air. The man, who was smoking a pipe, looked to be about

The area outside the Irish Club, where Steven Wagner encountered the apparition of an old man and his dog.

sixty years old and dressed in clothes that appeared to date from the 1940s. Beside him sat a small dog and both seemed to be looking blankly into the distance as if waiting for someone to arrive. The man wore a sad expression, and despite the presence of the dog he seemed a very solitary figure. Stephen, as one might expect, felt apprehensive and a little unnerved, and as the figure and the dog remained motionless he felt compelled to walk towards them. Yet, as he drew close, both suddenly vanished. The young man stopped in his tracks. Terrified, he ran back into the club to blurt out to his partying friends that he had just seen a ghost.

All laughed and said he had had too much to drink. He persuaded a few to go outside and look for the mysterious figure with the dog but, of course, the park area was deserted. Stephen was at a loss to explain what he had seen. Ribbing from his friends made him wonder if he did indeed imagine the whole event. Not wanting any more of the night's festivities he decided to go home, yet as he stepped once more out of the club he looked across to the small park area and, much to his amazement and shock, there again stood the figure of the old man with his dog by his side. Both remained in view for a few seconds before disappearing. At this, Stephen took to his heels not once looking back.

What are we to make of such an extraordinary incident? Once again such episodes leave more questions than answers: did Stephen observe a stone tape apparition? A crisis apparition? A phantasm of a living person, or a hallucination brought about by tiredness and one drink too many? Curiously, the small park area where the old man was seen was, between 1695 and 1913, a Quaker burial ground. The remains were removed when the piece of land was presented to the town. Is it possible that the apparition was once an occupant of the Quaker graveyard?

Because we cannot identify a phantom or the reasons for the presence, we run the risk of creating a persona and embellishing a paranormal incident with a host of invented add-ons. One such example that could lead to a ghost being created where none exist is an event that took place close to where Wagner saw the apparition, and has just the right amount of historical weight and added ghoulishness to furnish its own accompanying phantoms.

On 2 January 1736, Mr Pontifax, a Wycombe farmer, and his thirteen-year-old son left the Antelope Inn in the town after spending the evening with his sister-in-law, the landlady, Mrs Haydon. At about midnight he made his way home towards West Wycombe, but a mile outside the town he was accosted by two 'rogues' who shot and robbed him. Pontiflex's son managed to escape the attackers and raise the alarm. The men were arrested some weeks later at a London fair, and were tried for murder at Aylesbury. Early on the morning of 22 March 1736 they were brought by cart from Aylesbury to the Rye Common in Wycombe and were executed on an extraordinarily high gibbet. Such was the frenzy of interest in the event that the whole of the town turned out to view the spectacle, pushing over the wall of the Royal Grammar School in the crush to see the two men hanged. The corpses were left to rot and decay on the gibbet for four years before being cut down.

Our next port of call on our paranormal journey around Wycombe takes us to the most unlikely of ghostly settings; an ordinary suburban thoroughfare. Early one evening in October 1994, a young man was taking his dog for a walk down Totteridge Road, which is located just north-east of the centre of the town. As they turned the corner into Healy Avenue, the dog, who was off the lead, stopped and began to wag her tail. It was a clear, moonlit night, but there was nothing there that would account for her actions. As the owner watched he saw what appeared to be the shadow of

Healy Avenue, the site of a smiling, dog-loving phantom monk.

The following week he once again took his dog out for a walk. This time it was much later and there was no moon. As they went into Healy Avenue, the dog stopped and once more greeted her invisible friend. The strange encounter with the shadow occurred a month later but, this time things were different. Instead of a shadow the young man could clearly see a grey-haired figure wearing what appeared to be a monk's habit. The figure glided up to the dog, bent down, stroked her, then floated away and disappeared. Before the monk vanished the dog's owner had a good look at his face and declared it to be 'The kindest, friendliest face I have ever seen'.

a man bending down and stroking the dog. But there was nobody to go with the shadow. The dog refused to come when her owner called, so he had to go up and pull her away, at which point the shadow vanished.

We have already looked at the tape recording theories for ghosts, yet clearly these curious encounters would seem to question the stone tape hypothesis as a reason for phantoms. We may wonder how a paranormal recording, which is thought to endlessly repeat itself, can manipulate and act within the present. It would seem that the figure in the habit was as much aware of the dog and its owner as they were of him, and that what the man observed were the actions of a genuine ghost. Following the appearance of the grey-haired cleric other people have reported seeing the kind, dog-loving monk.

But why would the ghost of a monk, if the apparition was indeed a monk, choose to haunt a suburban area of Wycombe which has no history of a monastic establishment and, prior to housing development which began in the 1930s, was open farmland and fields? Wycombe's oldest building, apart from the parish church of All Saints', is the twelfth-century hospital building of St John the Baptist, the ruins of which still stand in Easton Street, and would have been administered by monks. Similarly, a thirteenth-century leper hospital which stood in what is now Green Street, or possibly on the site of Wycombe Abbey School, would have also had its sick tended to by Brothers of Mercy. Is it possible that a cleric from one of these establishments liked to occasionally find spiritual solitude in the fields and hills which would eventually become Healy Avenue?

Another of Wycombe's remnants from its medieval past is said to be haunted by a lady in white. Castle Hill House, an early seventeenth-century building, which is located in Priory Avenue in the centre of the town, stands within the grounds of an ancient motte and bailey castle which was besieged by King Stephen during the bloody anarchy between 1135 and 1157, when England was racked with civil war as Stephen tried to wrestle the crown from his cousin, Matilda. The outer bank of the bailey, which runs parallel with a modern brick wall along the avenue, is where the phantom is said to walk. She is believed to be a serving wench who worked for the Castle Hill estate. Her route takes her along what is now Priory Avenue to the flint stone cottage on Amersham Hill opposite Wycombe railway station. The flint cottage, before becoming a public house, was originally the lodge for Castle Hill House. Who the serving wench was, or how she came by her death, remain a mystery, though some say she was murdered in the house in the eighteenth century. On the upper floors of the house, which is now the Wycombe Museum, staff have experienced a sudden drop in temperature outside two of the rooms which were probably the living quarters of the serving staff back in its heyday.

If it is not the ghost of the unfortunate maid it might well be the phantom of a woman laid to rest

Castle Hill House (now the Wycombe Museum) is the site of a medieval castle and the spectre of a phantom woman.

Priory Avenue, where a female ghost is said to walk.

High Wycombe station, said to be haunted by the sounds of disembodied footsteps.

on the site long before the castle or the building came to be. In 1901, the skeleton of a young woman was unearthed from a barrow in the grounds of the house. The remains date from the early fifth or seventh century, and it is thought that she was the daughter of an Anglo-Saxon prince whose identity is now lost in the proverbial mists of time. Despite these colourful probabilities as to who the spectre is, plus the added romantic ingredient of secret passageways that are said to run between the house and the graveyard of All Saints' Church, we once again have virtually no contemporary eyewitness reports of the phantom lady in white.

Our last account of those Wycombe ghosts who prefer the open air to the town's ancient and modern buildings, begins one December in 1986 in the Flint Cottage pub. At 11.30, on a chilly, misty night, a British Rail employee was waiting for a train on platform 3 of High Wycombe station. He had been to a Christmas staff party at the Flint, and was returning to his home in Beaconsfield. The station was empty and quiet, yet as he stood under the cold glow of the platform lamps he heard the sound of approaching footsteps. They were not on the platform, but were coming from the ballast down on the track. He looked over at the track, expecting to see a railway worker walking along the line, but was astonished to see that the track was completely empty. As he listened, he distinctly heard the crunching noises passing by below him. At that moment, more people arrived on the station and during the momentary distraction the noises faded away.

A short while later he was talking with one of the members of staff at the station and mentioned what he had heard. He was rather surprised to discover that he was not the only one to have had the experience, as other people had also heard the footsteps along the track. The same staff member related that he had heard footsteps outside the station office and had gone to investigate, but there was no one there. The phantom footsteps crunching the ballast are not the only unusual things to be reported at the station. The frantic footfalls of someone running down the platform have been heard on several occasions, but on investigation there is nothing to account for them.

High Wycombe station is not unique in being a location where paranormal phenomena has been experienced. Indeed, the whole of Britain's railway network can boast a ghostly heritage just as varied and strange as our stately homes and castles. It is not surprising when one considers how impermanent life could be for those railway employees working on the hazardous permanent way. At Tulse Hill station in South London, the sound of disembodied footsteps has been heard walking along the platform on many occasions late at night before fading away into the tunnel.

Rather more alarmingly, one night in 1988 a maintenance worker inspecting the track between Finchely and Aldgate on the Northern Line in central London took time to rest in one of the many bolt holes along the tunnel when he heard the sound of footsteps crunching the ballast and coming towards him. He looked, expecting a fellow worker to appear, but the line was empty. Yet, much to his amazement and shock, as the footsteps passed him he could see the imprint of invisible boots depressing the ballast. The stunned maintenance man stared open-mouthed as the sound and impression of the disembodied footfalls continued along the track until they gradually diminished.

2

THE HAUNTED TOWN PART TWO

Houses, Hostelries and Public Buildings

WHEN you think of the words 'haunted house' a picture immediately springs to mind of an abandoned, gloomy, Gothic pile in a ruinous state, illuminated by the light of a full moon or the flash and crash of a dramatic thunderstorm. It is an enduring image which has its origin in the minds and creative works of the eighteenth- and nineteenth-century romantics. The ghosts and phantoms of the romantic imagination could flourish only within the towers, arches and gables of Gothic structures such as castles, churches and ivy-clad ruins. Perhaps the most classic haunted house of the last century was the infamous Borley Rectory, which stood on the border between Essex and Suffolk in eastern England. A twenty-three-room monstrosity, built in an ugly, domestic Gothic style in 1863, it witnessed all manner of paranormal phenomena before being consumed by flames in February 1939. It was demolished five years later, yet the lasting image of the gloomy rectory, photographed from the large, unkempt garden in which was located a pet cemetery and the path allegedly walked by a phantom nun, all add to the picture of what we think and expect a haunted house to be like.

But, of course, haunted houses come in many guises, and those which we will look at as we continue our journey through Wycombe's ghostly past are as varied and wide-ranging as one can imagine. We will come across not only the archetypal gloomy, Victorian Gothic house and stately mansion, but also the more humble suburban semi-detached house, the stalls of a newly built theatre, plus the gleaming glass and polished marble of a busy shopping centre.

Apart from our romantic castles and ancient churches, the next common location where ghosts are frequently reported is, perhaps, the public house. For centuries, pubs and inns have been the traditional meeting place for locals and travellers providing company, camaraderie and liquid sustenance for those seeking respite from the toils and troubles of the world. They are places where, over a pint of beer, stories are told, retold and embellished far beyond their origins. And ghost tales recounted over a last drink by the dying embers of a pub fire are no exception.

Many of Wycombe's pubs and inns have, no doubt, over the years, resounded to the telling of terrifying tales of things that go bump in the night or phantom, headless horsemen. Astonishingly, between 1750 and 1915, the town and its surrounding areas could boast, at one time or another, no less than 150 public houses: even as late as 1875 there still remained sixty-two in a town which was much smaller than the town of today.

Many of the hostelries have now sadly gone, but some of their stories of ghosts and phantoms remain. The Rose public house stood in Denmark Street, in a part of the town which now lies half-forgotten under the new Eden shopping centre. Many readers may remember enjoying a pint there, little knowing that the building was the scene of some unusual goings-on during 1983.

The pub seems to have had no history of paranormal phenomena prior to, or after the strange events of the early 1980s. My sister-in-law worked at The Rose as a barmaid, and on several occasions witnessed the figure of a woman in an upstairs storage room. The presence of the spirit was also felt in the bar late at night, when the room would go unnaturally cold. The landlord's two dogs would bark and shake with fear, and look into a corner of the bar seemingly terrified by an invisible presence. The identity of the woman is unknown, but it may well be the ghost of a former nanny, for the building was once a children's home. Is it possible that the woman disapproved of her former temperate home for orphans being turned into a place of intoxication?

Another of Wycombe's hostelries said to have a haunted reputation is the Hobgoblin, which stands in the centre of the town. Readers may well remember the pub when it was named the Three Tuns, and as the phenomena took place when the building was so called I will refer to it as such. It was built in 1756 as a coaching inn, and down the years the Three Tuns witnessed the coming and going of many thirsty travellers, especially during the late eighteenth and early nineteenth century when Wycombe rattled and clacked with the sound of wheels and hooves as coaches arrived

The Hobgoblin Inn, formerly the Three Tuns. (Courtesy of Rebecca Brazil)

over a year later there was the first visible manifestation. One day the landlord went into the room, and was rather shocked to see a vision of an old woman in a long blue dress sitting in the corner. The figure was hazy, but he could still make out that she had long fair hair and that she was brushing it. She appeared to be perched on a high stool, and as she sat, her black piercing eyes appeared to follow him round the room. At no point did he feel scared or alarmed, and he even felt that the ghost was in some way benevolent. The figure of the old woman was seen on many other occasions on almost every Sunday, and always in the oldest part of the building.

Curiously, following the regular Sunday appearance of the old woman, there were periods of apparent inactivity which seemed to follow the arrival of a newcomer to the pub's household. It was as if she had to accustom herself to someone new before once again showing herself. Although the woman did not make an appearance at this time, the sound of her footsteps in empty rooms upstairs was often heard in the pub not only by the landlords but also customers in the bar. Quite often she would reveal her presence by sudden cold draughts, lights switching themselves on and off and doors opening of their own accord. The pubs two dogs often seemed to react in markedly different ways to the phenomena. One would

to alight their passengers. Similar to The Rose, the Three Tuns seems to have had no previous history of the paranormal, although during its 250-year existence it may well have been the site of unexplained phenomena that was never recorded. Unexplained outbreaks of fire have occurred in the pub over the years.

In 1975, the pub was taken over by new landlords. The husband and wife team had only been in residence for a few weeks when things started to become strange. The landlord became aware of a presence and an unnatural chill in one of the upstairs bedrooms. The feelings persisted, but he refrained from telling his wife. Just growl and cringe in fear, while the other acted in playful recognition of an invisible friend.

To many people, ghosts are an object of fear, yet the phantom of the Three Tuns appears to be of the caring kind, for it seems one night she saved the life of a visitor to the pub. The guest spent the night in the room in which the ghost had been seen. The room was heated by a portable calor gas heater near the bed, and when the visitor went to sleep he left it on. This could have proved fatal as the close proximity of the heater to the bed could have resulted in a fire. Yet, on waking in the morning, he found that the heater had been turned off even though he insists he did not do it and neither did anyone else in the pub. Had the ghost helped avert a disaster? The spectre of the phantom woman has not been seen for some time, and although paranormal phenomena is still reported at the pub, it seems to be not of a benevolent kind, for bottles have been found smashed throughout the bar, and the staff fear going into the cellar alone because of an unsettling presence.

The Three Tuns is not Wycombe's only hostelry to have a reputation for weird happenings. The King George V on London Road is said to have strange shadows which appear on the walls of the bar. No matter how much people investigated the bizarre occurrences they could never find a physical reason for the phenomena. It is also said that after the pub has closed and the place locked up for the night, soft voices can be heard coming from within.

Another of Wycombe's haunted pubs is the Antelope. The present tavern, which stands adjacent to All Saints' Church in Church Square in the centre of the town, was built in 1795, and it was here, in 1798, that the Royal Military Academy was established before being moved to Sandhurst in Surrey in 1812. Tunnels are said to run beneath the pub, the entrance to which can be gained from the cellars. The purpose and extant of the subterranean passages has never been fully explored, but in 2005 a medium visiting the

The Antelope where a landlord was forced to flee in terror. (Courtesy of Rebecca Brazil)

pub asked to be shown the tunnels, and immediately sensed the presence of many spirits running throughout the passage ways. However, she could throw no light on who the spirits were, or the reason for their presence.

It's possible that the presence sensed by the medium in the tunnels might have chosen to manifest itself within the bar. In 2007, an ex-landlord of the Antelope had an unnerving experience when he was alone in the pub one night after closing time. Amazingly, the landlord's reaction was caught on CCTV and viewed by other members of the staff. The shaken boss, however, later rejected that he had been spooked by anything, and insisted that the tape be wiped. The footage showed him playing on one of the fruit machines in the empty pub when something caught his attention. He instantly swung around to see what it was, and then, without warning, suddenly bolted towards the front door seemingly in terror. When he was later asked about the incident he denied all knowledge of it, and forbade the staff to talk about the episode. Nonetheless, those who viewed the CCTV footage all agree that the landlord saw something which made him flee in fear from his own pub.

Another of Wycombe's hostelries to have a haunted reputation is the William Robert Loosley, which stands in Oxford Street in an area of the town which has seen much change and development in recent years. The pub was formerly the long-time premises of Hull, Loosley and Pearce, which was established in 1860 by the carpenter, builder, coffin maker and undertaker, William Robert Loosley. The building seems to have been free of paranormal phenomena during Loosley's time, yet since its remodelling as a public house disembodied footsteps have been heard on the upper floors by members of staff. Upon investigation there was nothing to account for them. The author's daughter worked at the pub for a time, and confirmed that the footsteps were heard by members of staff and that they sounded like the clomping tread of a heavy man. The opening and closing of doors on their own was also witnessed by staff members.

One night, after the pub had closed, a few staff were sat down relaxing and chatting around a table in the downstairs bar when they all heard one of the toilet doors swing violently open before banging shut. There was no one near the doors to open them in such an aggressive way, and on investigation the washroom was found to be empty. All are intriguing incidents but once again we are left with sporadic outbreaks of phenomena which, although puzzling, may well have rational explanations. They are included here as examples of the fleeting, incomprehensible and

The William Robert Loosley pub, said to haunted by strange footsteps. (Courtesy of Rebecca Brazil)

difficult-to-pin-down nature of ghosts and the paranormal.

Before we leave the William Robert Loosley we must make mention of a bizarre incident concerning Mr Loosley and the incredible events of 1871 when, according to the Wycombe businessman, a UFO landed in the town in the area of Plomer Hill. One night in October of that year, Loosley was standing in his garden to get some fresh air after waking with a slight fever. The time was 3 a.m., and on looking at the sky he saw what he thought was a star which seemed as if it was falling to earth with a great roar. In shock, he realised that the plummeting light was not a star but some kind of craft whose trajectory would bring it down on Plomer Hill in Downley. The craft disappeared from sight within the dark folds of the hills, but Loosley did not hear any sound of an impact.

The following day, he set out to find evidence of the craft which surely must have crashed to Earth. On reaching the site, Loosley found no sign of debris or evidence of any resulting fire, but did discover two unusually shaped metal objects that moved by themselves and made whizzing and whirring sounds. He says that they shone purple lights into his eyes where upon he could see amazing futuristic visions, including ghostly images of himself. Terrified, he fled the scene back to his home. Although he was totally shocked by what he had experienced he felt compelled to write down an account of the incident, stating: 'An account of a meeting with denizens of another world.' However, he was also aware that if knowledge of what he saw was made public he would be ridiculed and his reputation sullied, so he decided to hide his written account of what we would today call a UFO in a secret draw of a desk.

And there it apparently lay for a century before being discovered by his great-great-granddaughter, Edith Salter. Edith passed the written account of the UFO on to the science journalist and sci-fi writer David Frankland, who was given permission to publish it in a book he was writing on flying saucers. Frankland, was worried almost as much as Loosley that the account of the UFO would be debunked as the madness of a crank. He needn't have worried, for when the book was published in 1979, Loosley's story entered into UFO lore as an amazing and detailed account of what could only be explained as an alien visitation. And yet, the truth of the matter is that the whole story was a fraud perpetrated by Frankland as a practical joke played on believers and lovers of UFOs.

What is fascinating about Franklands hoodwink is that he chose to use an obscure High Wycombe businessman as central to his charade. He goes as far as acknowledging Loosley's granddaughter for her help, and also includes photos of Loosley's grave in Wycombe cemetery, and one of his shop on Oxford Road taken in the 1880s, which would become today's pub, to lend substance to his story. Strangely, the incident is still considered by uninformed authors as a true, first-hand account of a UFO sighting. Franklands hoax, however, is not unique.

In 1970, journalist Frank Smyth, who at the time was an associate editor of *Man, Myth and Magic* magazine, set out to see if he could invent a ghost, and what response it would generate. He therefore created the 'Mad Vicar of Ratcliffe Wharf in London'. The article appeared in the 1970 summer edition of the magazine, and claimed that an eighteenth-century clergyman from St Anne's Church on the Isle of Dogs, who owned a boarding house in the area, was in the habit of murdering his guests, robbing them and disposing their bodies in the Thames. The vicar was apprehended and executed, and since then his ghost has been reported walking the streets of Limehouse. Incredibly, the story quickly became East End folklore with people claiming to have seen the ghost, and within a year eight separate books had been written about the fictitious phantom, some even embellishing the story. Smyth eventually admitted the deception and sightings of the vicar ceased.

The reason for including both the Plomer Hill UFO and the Vicar of Wapping stories here is to demonstrate how the most fragile and flimsy accounts of ghosts and phantoms can sometimes be given credibility and truth simply by appearing on the printed page or, more tellingly, on today's seemingly unquestioning internet. However, despite the widespread refutation of the Ratcliffe spook, one paranormal investigator has suggested that Smyth's ghost may well have existed after all, and that it somehow made itself known to him via his imagination.

Following our brief, spurious detour into outer space we now return to earth in the centre of the town. Not all of Wycombe's ghosts are to be found in its attractive half-timbered Georgian-fronted buildings. The strikingly designed Wycombe Swan Theatre opened its doors in November 1992. In 1998, fifty-year-old ex-fireman Bob Eastland became caretaker and one of his duties was to secure the premises after all of the staff had left. One night, after he had been in the job for six months, he was crossing the auditorium when he had an extraordinary and unnerving experience. As it was 11 p.m., the auditorium was lit only by minimal lighting, yet there was enough for Bob to see by as he crossed

the Dress Circle. Much to his surprise he saw someone sitting in one of the seats. He was curious, because at the time he should have been the only person in the building. Thinking that it was either someone who had fallen asleep, or become unwell, he made his way across to where they were sitting. However, on reaching the person, he got the shock of his life for the figure vanished right in front of his eyes. Bob was to later learn that other members of staff and players on the stage had also seen the unknown figure. Following Bob's initial sighting he didn't see the apparition again, yet he says he was always aware of an invisible presence, which followed him when he was alone at night in the theatre.

Some years later, he was assigned a young assistant named Tom Schoon. One evening in 2006, when the theatre was closing for the night, Tom was asked to complete the locking up by himself whilst Bob remained at the stage door. After a while, Bob decided to help out by locking the doors and turning off the lights in the band pit and downstairs area. When he returned to the stage door he radioed Tom and informed him what he had done, but the young assistant replied saying that wasn't possible, as the doors were open and the lights were on.

To try and unravel the uncanny happenings, the manager of the theatre asked blind medium Sharon Neill to use her abilities to see if the

The Wycombe Swan Theatre, where a phantom figure has been seen sitting in the auditorium.

building was haunted and by whom. Neill began her examination of the theatre in the auditorium, where the phantom figure had been seen by the staff. Yet, she was soon compelled to find her way, with her manager's assistance, through the labyrinth of rooms and corridors which link the Swan Theatre to an adjoining room in the Town Hall, and in particular the first chamber of the oak room. On entering the room, Neill immediately detected a presence. However, she soon became aware that there was another smaller room off the main chamber, and pointed directly to its double doors. She was led through the doors, but stopped just in front of the bar area. Once again, she detected a presence which was not visible to those around her. She described it as a man in his late forties or fifties, and dressed in a double-breasted suit with a white shirt. She went on to say that there was also a second person which she could feel: a domestic woman wearing an apron, whose hair was tied back into a little bun. The woman appeared to be friendly, but the man was angry at the way the oak room was now being used. Neill asked if the tablecloths in the function room were pulled to the ground regularly, with no reason as to why. One of the team accompanying Neill confirmed that the catering staff had regularly reported that gold and white tablecloths, which had been laid in place, had been found inexplicably crumpled on the floor. Neill thought that the presence of the man was the spirit of a former Major of Wycombe by the name of Williams.

It is probable that Neill does indeed possess some kind of mediumistic ability, although it is difficult to confirm with any certainty that the presence she felt whilst in the oak room was the ghost of the former major, or indeed that the phantom was that which had been seen in the auditorium of the theatre. Nonetheless, a previous caretaker of the Town Hall reported that he had seen the ghost of a woman dressed in Tudor clothing strolling between the pillars in the Oak Room. He recalled, as had Neill, that she was friendly. It is likely that the caretaker mistook the attire of the phantom domestic woman he saw as being Elizabethan for the oak room was built in the late nineteenth century, 400 years after the close of the Tudor period.

Another building in Wycombe where paranormal phenomena has been reported is the Octagon shopping centre. Although it would seem to be the most unlikeliest place to find such a phantom, one day in October 1988, around 8 a.m., a group of school friends were walking through the centre when one of their number, who was a little behind the others,

chanced to look up at the gallery, which runs the length of the store, and saw someone walking along the balcony. The figure was grey and, to the witness, resembled a monk in a cowled habit. The young woman could hardly believe her eyes as she watched the form slowly glide along the gallery and then fade from view. She excitedly shouted at her friends to look up, but when they did, the apparition had vanished. Of course, we must ask, what was the ghost of a monk, if indeed it was so, doing in a modern shopping centre that was constructed in the early 1970s?

Curiously, another of Wycombe's shopping centres has also been the site of paranormal phenomena. The Chilterns opened its doors in May 1988 as a rival to the large Octagon. Its north side opens out on to Frogmore, near the site of the palace cinema. It was in one of the retail units on this side of the centre that staff reported many unexplained incidents which included disembodied footsteps, voices, the movement of objects and the appearance of apparitions. The shop's storeroom in particular was an area the staff refused to be alone in. Reports of the phenomena seemed to have waxed and waned and by the late 1990s had virtually ceased. The reasons for the disturbances are unknown and it would appear to be another example of the fleeting and ungraspable nature of ghostly phenomena. During the

The entrance to the Chilterns shopping mall in Frogmore, built on the site of a seventeenth-century house of correction. The closed retail unit on the right was the scene of paranormal phenomena during the early 1990s. (Courtesy of Rebecca Brazil)

termed it a 'loathsome dungeon' – one wonders how many of its inmates perished within its walls before gaining their freedom. The prison also served as a home for maimed soldiers. In April 1794, a crack cavalry regiment was quartered in Wycombe under the command of a General Gwynne. At the time, it was in a state of near mutiny due to the barbaric treatment meted out to the men by order of a Major Shadwell. One trooper, who was mercilessly flogged, committed suicide within the house of correction.

research for this book the author visited the shop to see if the present staff had experienced anything unusual. Sadly, the unit, like most of the outlets in the Chilterns, is closed and boarded up. It has become, ironically, a haunted premises standing in the ghost of a shopping centre.

The strange incidents that were reported in the Chilterns may well find their origins in a building which once stood on the site. In 1659, a house of correction was erected on Frogmore to replace the old gaol under the guildhall. It was not a pleasant place, for when a group of Quakers were imprisoned there in 1665 they

It would seem that one can come upon a ghost in practically any circumstance or location. We have already encountered phantoms in public houses, theatres, shopping malls, prisons and railway stations, yet the humble semi-detached house is a setting where we can just as easily experience a ghost as one would in the stateliest of stately abodes. But, it would seem that to experience the paranormal in the 'ordinariness' of the family home only serves to make the phenomena more personal, and therefore all the more alarming. Perhaps a good example is the Enfield poltergeist in which a mother and her four children living in an ordinary north London semi in 1977 were, for eighteen months, subjected to the actions of a violent poltergeist.

Of course, there are also particular paranormal incidents which are all the more disturbing for occurring in a domestic setting. It is a peculiar aspect of some hauntings that those ghosts which appear to cause the most fear to those who encounter them are of people, who, when in life, are considered to be the weakest and most vulnerable in society; namely young children.

In April 1992, Andrew MacLean and his wife, Jan, moved into No. 180 Bowerdean Road, which lies just outside of the centre of Wycombe. For the first few months of their tenancy they experienced nothing out of the ordinary, and life continued in its

The house on Bowerdean Road, where Jan and Andrew MacLean heard the eerie cry of invisible babies.

regular, everyday fashion. One night, however, Mr MacLean was awakened by what he described as two young children or babies crying. At first, he thought that the sounds were coming from the house next door, but realised they couldn't be, as his neighbours were an elderly couple in their late seventies. Sitting up in bed, he listened; the sounds of the crying children seemed to be coming from the room below. As his wife slept peacefully beside him, Mr MacLean got out of bed and, somewhat hesitantly, went downstairs to the living room. When he switched on the light, the crying abruptly ceased. Puzzled, he inspected the house but could find nothing to account for the sound of the distraught children. Stepping outside the front door, he explored around the rear of the building and up the garden but all was quiet. Mr MacLean continued to hear the sounds of the crying babies on and off for the next few weeks, but refrained from telling his wife for fear of alarming her. But she had also heard the babies and had likewise held back from telling her husband. On several occasions, whilst alone at night, Mrs MacLean heard the sound of the distraught infants coming from an upstairs bedroom. Reluctantly she climbed the stairs to the room, yet, on entering and switching on the light, the crying stopped.

After some time, the sounds of the crying babies began to play on the

MacLeans' nerves. They wondered, apprehensively, if the eerie sounds foreshadowed some bad future event. Curiously, the sounds would cease for long periods only to return as unexpectedly as they had begun. At times, after the couple had spent the night out socialising, they would return home to find all the lights in the house on. Even when the MacLeans' went away on holiday, friends, who they had asked to keep an eye on their home, often thought the couple had returned early as they found every room in the building lit up. So much was the stress caused by the bizarre phenomena that the MacLean's thought seriously of asking the local authority to rehouse them. Yet, just as unexpectedly as the crying had started it ceased all together, and to this date has not returned.

There is a curious footnote to this story and one which would seem to echo the experience of Michael Powell and the sound of children which were heard in Pugh's Wood. The MacLean's were to discover that prior to their tenancy of 180 Bowerdean Road the house had been rented by a Scottish couple who lived there with their three young children. However, Mr and Mrs MacLean were shocked to learn that some years before the Scottish couple became the proud parents of three healthy kids, two of their children had tragically died in infancy in the house. More puzzling is that at another property, two doors

Hughenden Manor, former home of Victorian statesman, Benjamin Disraeli.

away from the MacLean's home, a second family also suffered the trauma of losing two children at birth.

From ghosts in modern locations we now move on to the site of Hughenden Manor, which stands just outside the centre of Wycombe. This grand stately pile was the former home of Victorian politician and statesman, Benjamin Disraeli. The house was built in the late eighteenth century, but it is possible that a building has existed on the site since the eleventh century. The manor of Hughenden is first recorded in 1086, when it was assessed for tax at a cost of ten hides. The name is probably derived from an old English personal name, Huhha or Hucca and Denu meaning Huhhas Valley. During the Second World War, the house was used as a secret intelligence base, code-named 'Hillside', where Air Ministry staff analysed aerial photography of Germany and created maps for bombing missions, including the famous Dambusters raid in 1943.

Victorian statesman and politician, Benjamin Disraeli, who is said to haunt his former home, Hughenden Manor. (Author's Collection)

the house, one of the team wandered away from the main party into the study. She was examining a painting when, out of the corner of her eye, she caught a movement. Turning, she saw the ghost of Disraeli staring at her.

On other occasions, the wraith of Disraeli has been seen on the main staircase with papers in his hand. The stairs seem to have been one of his more favoured spots, for another female visitor once came upon him standing near the portrait of himself that stands on the staircase. She reported that the ghost stood for a time, oblivious or unaware of her presence, and then, as approaching voices were heard, it dissolved.

Paranormal aromas have also been smelt at Hughenden. On several occasions, members of staff, on entering a study which contains Disraeli's peers robes, shoes and sword, have distinctly smelt the scent of perfume or cologne. The politician, who was looked upon as a dandy, often dressed in flamboyant clothes and wore the Victorian equivalent of aftershave.

The ghost of Disraeli is not the only phantom that is thought to walk at Hughenden. The woods to the rear are said to be haunted by the ghost of a young woman who died in mysterious circumstances. Anyone unlucky enough to encounter her will be forever pursued by her spirit. Perhaps it is not surprising that this ancient and stately location has its spooks.

Disraeli, who was a favourite of Queen Victoria, became Prime Minister in 1868, and again between 1874 and 1880. He purchased the house in 1848 with a loan of £25,000 (equivalent to almost £1,500,000 today) from two political allies. The manor was remodelled in the Gothic style, and it remained the statesman's home until his death in 1881

It was soon after his death that reports that his ghost had been seen walking the rooms and staircase of the house began to circulate, and have continued to do so. Among those who have claimed to have witnessed the spectre was a visiting member of the Ghost Club, Britain's oldest psychical research organisation. During a tour of

A centuries old path is said to wind its way from Naphill down through the woods to Hughenden Church. Known as the coffin road, it was the route by which the dead were taken for burial in the graveyard of St Michael's Church.

We now move a few miles south of Hughenden Manor to a more humble haunted location. In 1949, the Battison family moved into a cottage on Brimmers Hill in Widmer End, which stands halfway between Hazlemere and the outskirts of Wycombe at Terriers. The dwelling is an attractive white-stone detached building, possibly dating back to the eighteenth century. During their five-year tenancy, the family were repeatedly disturbed by strange noises. Mrs Battison was the first to experience the phenomena one afternoon as she lay on her bed for a short rest. The time was 1 p.m., and as she dozed she distinctly heard footsteps coming up the stairs. At first she thought it was one of her dogs, and then she was not so sure, as the tread was heavy and pronounced. She listened and the footsteps seemed to reach the top of the stairs and stop. Mrs Battison listened but there was no sound coming from the landing. Suddenly, she was jolted from her slumbers by a tremendous clamour in another bedroom. After a while the noise seemed to enter the room in which she lay and made its way across the floor to a large wardrobe that stood against the far wall. Incredibly the sound, or whatever was making it, appeared to enter the wardrobe. The racket eventually ceased, and when Mrs Battison finally plucked up the courage to open the door of the closet, she found it to be empty.

Following on from this bizarre episode, the family would regularly hear a tremendous banging noise coming from one of the bedrooms. This frequently happened around midday when they were all sitting in the kitchen having lunch. Whenever they went to investigate, the noise would cease as they reached the bedroom door. On one occasion a friend, who was staying with the family and who had been warned about the strange sounds, scoffed at the notion that the house was haunted. To show he was unconcerned about ghosts he chose to stay alone in the house while the Battisons went away for the weekend. On the families return, however, they found that their guest had fled the cottage, vowing never to spend another second there. He refrained from sharing his experience, only to inform the Battisons that his views on the paranormal had changed.

Loud knocks were also heard on the back door in the evening. Initially it was thought that someone was playing a prank, so the family tried to apprehend the perpetrator but to no avail. Footsteps were also heard overhead, and the dogs would listen at the back door and follow something invisible across the room with their eyes. Unseen hands would lift the catches on the doors and they would swing open by themselves.

After the Battisons had left the house it changed hands several times with the new residents seemingly forced out by unseen presences: one family fled in panic after only a few days. Another, who had employed an *au pair*, left the house after the terrified girl tried to jump out of a window when she encountered the apparition of an old man. A couple who lived there for a short period would often come down to breakfast in the morning to find the kitchen light bulb on the table. No explanation for the strange disturbances was immediately forthcoming, although they did subsequently diminish. However, it later came to light that some years before the Battissons took up residence at the

cottage a previous owner, following his wife's death, became a recluse, shunning friends and family and never leaving the house. He eventually committed suicide in the back bedroom.

An intriguing addition to the Widmer End haunting was discovered during research for this book. The author's aunt, as a young woman, had known the Battison family, and even though she herself never visited the cottage, or indeed was aware of the strange events occurring there, her parents would often take care of the property when the family went away. On several occasions when they were staying at the house, knocks were heard at the front door, but on opening it there was no one there. Many times on leaving the cottage, her father had the unnerving sensation of being followed along the road. He heard footstops walking behind him, but on turning around found that the road was empty. Today, the cottage remains at peace, for no disturbances have been reported for several years.

3

THE PHANTOMS OF WEST WYCOMBE

WEST Wycombe is deserving of its own chapter in this book as it can boast not only eight spectres, but it is also the site of the meeting place of the notorious Knights of St Francis, better known to us today as 'The Hellfire Club'.

The village of West Wycombe lies some two and a half miles from the centre of High Wycombe along the A40. It is a pleasing location containing many fine half-timbered buildings dating from the fifteenth to eighteenth centuries, and even though today it is somewhat marred by the traffic which thunders along its high street, the alleys, lanes and courtyards off the main thoroughfare still retains an air of quiet calm. The village is saved from the urban creep of High Wycombe by the boundary at the pedestal junction where the A4010 branches from the A40 to head north to Aylesbury. The effect is immediate; the houses, shops and petrol stations of the town sprawl abruptly cease, and the village and the Chiltern countryside commences.

It is here, in this rural charm, that ghosts, murder, pagan worship and the debauchery of eighteenth-century titled gentry are all inextricably linked with this seemingly peaceful English village, its church, which stands proudly on top of West Wycombe Hill, and the infamous activities that are said to have taken place within the labyrinth of caves which snake their way beneath. Of all the haunted locations contained within this book, West Wycombe could well be described as a place perfect for ghosts and the mysteries of Britain's pagan past. The hilltop site of West Wycombe's parish church, dedicated to St Lawrence, the patron saint of prostitutes, readily deserves the description of 'spectacular'.

Standing within the ramparts of an Iron-Age hill fort, the church looks

West Wycombe Hill.

out over the grand sweep and roll of the Chiltern Hills. The site has been continuously occupied for thousands of years. A Bronze Age settlement is widely believed to have first existed on the hill, and research has shown that a Pagan temple was constructed here, in a similar style to Stonehenge. The Romans also built their own settlement and religious temple here. During the Saxon period the site became the village of Haeferingdune, the 'Hill of Haefer's People', a name which later evolved into Haveringdon. The hill retained its religious importance and the first Christian church was erected there in AD 635.

The population at Haveringdon was greatly reduced by the Black Death in the fourteenth century, and by the early eighteenth century the village had relocated to the valley along the Oxford Road and was subsequently renamed, due to its position west of the town of High Wycombe, with the villagers retaining St Lawrence as their parish church. The name West Wycombe is recorded as early as 1195, and it is probable that a settlement existed on the site of today's village as far back as the eleventh century. Today, no trace of Haveringdon village on the hill survives. With such an ancient and dark past it seems appropriate that the one man who would become synonymous with West Wycombe took eagerly to the pleasures, rituals and rakish delights of eighteenth-century decadence.

In 1724, Sir Francis Dashwood (1708–1781), 2nd Baronet, and later 15th Baron le Despencer, succeeded to the estate and set about remodelling the house, West Wycombe Park. Like many titled gentlemen of his day he embarked on a grand tour of Europe and returned to England with his own grandiose plans for West Wycombe. The house, built and added to between 1740 and 1800, was conceived as a pleasure palace for an eighteenth-century libertine. The building encapsulates the entire progression of British eighteenth-century architecture from Palladian to Neoclassical, and is set within a landscaped park containing temples and follies.

The Baronet didn't limit his ideas and plans to just his home and gardens. In 1751, the fourteenth-century church of St Lawrence disappeared within Dashwood's rebuilding of the interior,

Sir Francis Dashwood. (Author's collection)

copied on the third-century Temple of the Sun at Palmyra, in Damascus. Only the medieval tower was retained, which itself was considerably heightened and topped by a great golden ball fitted with benches, large enough to contain six people. It was in the golden ball that Dashwood and his cronies drank the night away as they played cards and related bawdy tales. In 1765, the vast hexagonal Dashwood mausoleum was built to the east of the church. Its design was derived from the Constantine Arch in Rome, and it was where the Dashwood memorials would be erected.

Yet, of all Sir Francis' grand schemes for West Wycombe perhaps the most ambitious was undertaken between 1748 and 1752, with the extension of a series of ancient chalk tunnels under West Wycombe Hill into an elaborate labyrinth of caves and chambers. In order to provide work for the unemployed, following a succession of harvest failures, Dashwood paid each labourer a shilling per day to excavate the passageways which extended a third of a mile into the hill. Although it was a generous show of altruism, the Baronet had other motives. The cave's designs were much inspired by Dashwood's travels in the Mediterranean. The descent through the passageways and underground chambers concluded by crossing a subterranean river named the Styx, and entering into the inner temple which is said to lie directly 300ft below the church of St Lawrence. According to Greek mythology the River Styx separated the mortal world from the immortal world, and the subterranean position of the Inner Temple directly beneath Saint Lawrence's Church was supposed to signify Heaven and Hell.

Between 1750 and 1766, the Hellfire Club held their nefarious meetings in the caves below the hill. Although their drunken gatherings took place at the ruined Medmenham Abbey situated on the banks of the River Thames, 8 miles south of West Wycombe. Here they called themselves the 'Monks of Medmenham', and their numbers included artist William Hogarth, political activist John Wilkes, John Montague, 4th Earl of Sandwich, poet Paul Whitehead and possibly, at times, Benjamin Franklin. It is uncertain what exactly the Hellfire Club members got up to during their twice monthly meetings in the caves. They greeted each other as Brother and dressed as monks, while their accompanying ladies were attired as virginal nuns. Possibly some form of Satanic or Pagan ritual mimicry took place, but more likely they indulged in drinking, gambling and whoring. The Club disbanded in recrimination in 1766, following a practical jape played on the Earl of Sandwich during one of their drunken ceremonies, and his

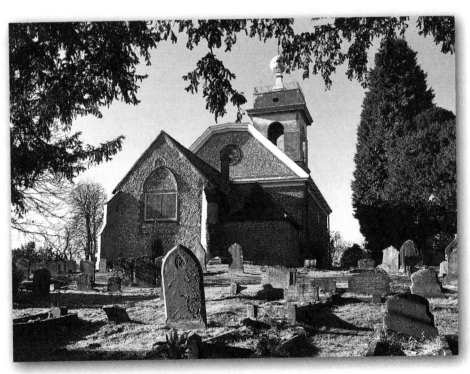

St Lawrence's Church on West Wycombe Hill.

Above: *The Dashwood Mausoleum on West Wycombe Hill, where the ghost of Paul Whitehead is said to walk.*

Right: *Paul Whitehead. (Author's collection)*

subsequent ridicule for believing that the materialisation of a monkey, jokingly released from a box by a fellow member, was the manifestation of the Devil.

Following Dashwood's death in 1781, the caves fell out of use and became derelict. It was in the early nineteenth century that the subterranean passageways and West Wycombe Hill became the site of reported ghostly phenomena. Paul Whitehead, a steward and secretary of the Hellfire Club and close friend to Sir Francis Dashwood, had his heart placed in an elegant marble urn in the mausoleum, as his will requested. (The rest of his remains were buried at St Mary's Church in Twickenham, just outside London.) In 1829, it was allegedly stolen by an Australian soldier, and it is believed that the ghost of Whitehead haunts the caves and West Wycombe Hill, searching for his heart.

Numerous visitors and staff have reported seeing a man in old-fashioned clothing wandering the cave passageways. When seen, he is said to vanish into thin air. A young girl visiting the caves became separated from her friends and found she was alone in a deep part of the labyrinth. Not seeing or hearing any other person, she began to feel lost and frightened. The atmosphere within the caves was changing, becoming cold and dim. Feeling that she must find her way to the exit, she quickly returned along a passageway which seemed to ascend towards the entrance. She had only gone a short distance when she became aware that someone was following her. Turning, she saw the figure of a man in eighteenth-century clothing standing some distance away staring at her. As they faced each other, the young woman said she felt in no way threatened by the man and assumed he was one of the caves' living history guides. But, as she looked the figure gradually faded away.

Perhaps the most well known and frequently sighted ghost to walk the caves, as well as the George and Dragon pub in the village, is that of Suki, an attractive sixteen-year-old barmaid employed at the pub during the late eighteenth century. It was said that she fell for the charms of a gentleman who was passing through the village, much to the annoyance of three local lads who also had their eye on the pretty serving girl. A message, purporting to be from the handsome gentleman, was sent to Suki at the tavern, instructing her to meet him in the caves at night. Dressed in her finest white dress she entered the caves only to find that the message had been a hoax planned by the three jealous boys. In anger she threw rocks at the laughing lads. When the boys responded by throwing rocks back, Suki was knocked unconscious. She was secretly brought back to her room at the inn but the next morning she was found dead. Her ghost is said to walk the corridors of the George, and has also been reported to glide across the garden.

In 1967, an American tourist staying at the George was intrigued by the story of the ghostly barmaid and wanted to sleep in the reportedly haunted room. Part way through the night he awoke with a start as he felt icy hands placed on his forehead. When he turned on the lamp the feeling went away and the room was empty. Then he noticed a pinpoint of light near the door. As he watched, it grew in length and width. It had a strange, opaque, almost pearly quality and would vanish when he switched the light on, only to reappear when he turned it off. Gathering courage he went over to the light, but as soon as he reached it he felt the most intense cold, and he couldn't breathe and his limbs felt heavy. Suddenly the illuminated form moved towards him and he leapt back in terror onto the bed, turning on the light as he did so. At once the strange shape vanished. So much was the American's fear at what he had experienced he slept no more that

The George and Dragon pub, West Wycombe, said to be haunted by murdered barmaid, Suki.

night and left early the next morning, vowing never to spend another second at the George.

The spectre of Suki has also been seen looking from the windows of the inn waiting and pining for her lost love. In the early 1990s, the landlady of the George entered one of the rooms and saw the apparition of a young woman with a sad, lost expression sitting by the fire. After a few moments the ghost turned to look at the landlady and then slowly faded away.

The phantom barmaid is not the only ghost said to walk the rooms and corridors at the pub. Disembodied footsteps have been heard descending the main staircase and are believed to be the spirit of a visitor to the inn who was robbed and murdered in his room during the eighteenth century.

The paranormal activity at West Wycombe is not only confined to the George and Dragon pub. In 1995, five teenage girls were camping near woodland on West Wycombe Hill. At about 1 a.m., they were awoken by the sound of what they described as howling, which seemed to surround the tent. The terrified girls listened

The main staircase at the George and Dragon, haunted by disembodied footsteps.

as the strange, guttural cry continued for several minutes before suddenly stopping. Their frightening ordeal had not ceased, however, as the tent was then lit up by flashing lights from outside. Although extremely alarmed at what was happening, two of the teenagers plucked up enough courage to pull back the flaps and peer outside. At once the flashing lights were extinguished and the hill was in darkness. All the girls now frantically exited the tent to see what was going on but, as they did so, the terrifying howling started once again. The strange sounds continued for a few seconds and again abruptly ceased. As the trembling teenagers clung to each other for comfort, they at once all heard the approaching heavy thud of a horse in full gallop. To the young women's astonishment and terror, there appeared from nowhere the apparition of a headless man riding a white horse, which sped across the field close to where they stood. The girls watched open-mouthed as the horse and rider continued up the hill. Yet, even though they could hear the sounds of hooves on earth, the white horse seemed to be galloping a metre above the ground. Just as quickly as the speeding horse had appeared it vanished into the darkness and the sound of the hooves faded away. The experience was too much for the five teenagers and they hastily broke down their tent and fled.

What are we to make of such an incredible story? It would seem that the paranormal incident, or incidents, give the impression of being in some way scripted, beginning with the howling, followed by flashing lights and climaxing with the appearance of a headless rider on a phantom horse. All three features of the phenomena are dissimilar, and we may wonder in what way they are connected. A sceptic might easily point out that the howling sounds could have been the natural cries of a nocturnal creature; a sound unfamiliar to the teenagers and in the darkness interpreted as something threatening. Similarly, the flashing lights can be explained as the headlights of cars shining from a distance and then moving on. But what of the phantom horse and rider? Once again, the sceptic could argue that the girls were in an alarmed and impressionable state and were, therefore, primed to regard anything strange or unusual that they observed in the darkness as paranormal.

There is, however, a tradition at West Wycombe that on moonlit nights the ghost of Sir Francis Dashwood rides up the hill on a brilliant white charger. Unlike the rider experienced by the five teenagers, Sir Francis is not without his head as he gallops towards the church of St Lawrence. But did the youngsters really observe the ghost of Dashwood? What we may have here is another case of a possible genuine paranormal incident that has been witnessed over the years, and the unknown apparition or paranormal anomaly assigned an identity; in this case, Sir Francis Dashwood.

West Wycombe House is also not without its ghosts. The music room is said to be haunted by a lady in white who is thought be the grandmother of Sir Francis Dashwood. The ghost of a phantom monk has also been seen in the room. When celebrated playwright and songwriter, Noel Coward was staying at the house he gave a recital in the music room. As he played the piano he saw the figure of a smiling monk watching him. With typical nonchalance and without the least hint of alarm, Coward continued his song to the end, after which the smiling, and no doubt appreciative, brother disappeared.

Smiling monks, headless horsemen, ladies in white and phantom barmaids, West Wycombe would seem to have them all. Yet how do we explain such phenomena? One theory that might explain the paranormal anomalies that have been experienced on West Wycombe Hill, and indeed within the caves below, was proposed by parapsychologist T.C. Lethbridge, and may well give clues as to why people encounter ghosts in churches and at sites chosen for the construction of ancient monuments such as Stonehenge, the Avebury stone circle in Wiltshire and indeed West Wycombe Hill.

West Wycombe House.

In 1923, Alfred Watkins, a Herefordshire brewer, put forward the now familiar theory that sites such as standing stones, tumuli, hilltops and churches were all connected by a system of 'ley' lines that could be established by dowsing. Lethbridge expanded Watkins' concept and held the view that Christian churches were built at a chosen location not only as a way of converting those who were still attached to the old pagan beliefs, but because it was recognised in pre-scientific days that the ground itself was 'sacred'. The countless stone circles and ancient places of worship scattered throughout Britain are sites where Lethbridge, who was an expert dowser, detected powerful forces very much like an electric current. He theorised that ancient priests and holy men had recognised this Earth force and ordered the buildings to be placed there to absorb and conduct the power. Lethbridge also proposed that this earth energy or magnetism could in some way act as a psychic recorder of emotional vibrations of events that have taken place. They could be negative or positive emotions and, on occasion, so strong that they can be picked up by sensitive people who visit a particular site and who experience psychic phenomena, seemingly sounds and images of incidents that occurred many centuries before. This theory is similar, as we have already noted, to Lethbridge's idea that a damp atmosphere can also record emotions and play them back to a suitably sensitive person. He also postulated that it was the power of the Earth's magnetism that could enhance the mind and aid a person's consciousness to experience paranormal phenomena. Whatever the theories, they remain, as do most of the explanations for ghosts and phantoms, conjecture.

Nonetheless, the atmosphere of the past hangs heavy over West Wycombe Hill and village with the fingerprints of all who have left their mark. Then again there may well be a far more simple and obvious reason as to why ghosts have been reported at West Wycombe. Eighty years before Sir Francis Dashwood was born, Roundhead soldiers of the Parliamentary army marching through the village would have defaced and destroyed any images, statues or iconography they found in St Lawrence's Church as superstitious idolatry and unchristian. In 1754, the Baronet Sir Francis Dashwood remodelled a Christian building in the guise of a Pagan temple, and below, created his own playground Hades – a breeding ground for the paranormal perhaps?

4

GHOSTS IN THE CHILTERNS

Amersham

Amersham is really two places. The new town on the hill is a product of Metro land, so beloved of poet laureate, Sir John Betjeman. With the extension of the metropolitan railway in the early 1900s, Amersham on the Hill expanded to accommodate the growing number of commuters who travelled daily to London. By contrast, the old town a mile south is a different place altogether. The high street is lined with a host of fine buildings dating from the fourteenth to the eighteenth centuries, and its many courtyards and inns remind us of a time when the town was a stopping place on the old coaching route from London to Aylesbury and the north. Indeed, it would seem that Amersham has an abundance of haunted hostelries, which include the Saracens Head where the ghost of a seventeenth-century serving wench is said to haunt the building. There is also the Griffin (now converted to a pizza bar) where the ghost of a horn-blowing coachman, who once had the honour of driving King George VI, and who regularly celebrated the anniversary of his special day by drinking himself into a stupor and blowing his horn out of tune in the courtyard of the inn. When the coachman retired, the landlord of the Griffin allowed him to continue to celebrate his yearly day of fame, but insisted he didn't play his horn. However, after the coachman died it was said that the sound of his phantom horn could be heard blaring again in the courtyard of the pub.

The Chequers Inn
The Chequers public house, which stands in London Road, dates from the fifteenth century. It is said that several ghosts haunt the building, including

a shrieking woman and two cloaked and hooded figures. During the early sixteenth century, seven men, who were 'lollards' (religious dissenters), were burned at the stake in Amersham on charges of heresy, and it is believed that they were held in the inn prior to their execution. Over the years, the paranormal happenings at the pub have forced at least one landlord to flee in terror after the sounds of a screaming woman were heard by his family. His daughter also reported seeing the apparition of a hooded figure in her bedroom.

In 1971, a barman working at the pub encountered the ghost of a man wearing a long cloak. Locals believe that this was the spectre of Mr Osman, a warder who had accompanied the seven condemned men the night before they went to the stake. It is thought by many ghost hunters who have researched the case, that the shrieking woman, who has terrified many of the pubs tenants, is Joan Clerke, daughter of William Tyslworth, one of the executed men. Another ghostly woman, clad in grey, is said to haunt the road outside the inn. Apart from the appearance of apparitions, other phenomena experienced at the Chequers include sudden drops in temperature and the landlord's pets becoming agitated and frightened.

The haunting of the pub dates back decades, and would seem to have become seriously disturbing for the tenants. There have been three exorcisms recorded at the pub, taking place in 1953, 1963 and again in 1982. Yet it would appear these were unsuccessful, as an unseen presence is still felt at the inn today.

The Crown Hotel

The Crown Inn, now named the Crown Hotel, was originally an old coaching inn, dating back to the sixteenth or seventeenth century. Down the years the hotel has been visited by a number of Britain's rich and famous personalities, including Lord Protector Oliver Cromwell in the seventeenth century, to 1950s British screen heart-throb Dirk Bogarde. On a number of occasions the apparition of a figure has apparently been seen leaning against one of the old posts in the bar room when it has been empty of customers. Further reports tell of the ghost of a serving girl appearing in one of the bedrooms, and of a woman who is said to climb the stairs before disappearing through a door. Within the pub's oldest rooms, guests have woken suddenly in the night with the sensation of an electric shock passing through their body. Incredibly, the pub is said to house

The Crown Hotel, Amersham, where the kindly ghost of a chambermaid tucks in the covers of sleeping guests.

seven ghosts, including a Victorian housekeeper who tucks the guests into their beds. It is believed that she appears during the Easter period, and even though her concern for the comfort of those staying at the inn might seem to be a benevolent ghostly service, it was too much for three burly men who fled from their rooms at 3 a.m., after they felt phantom hands tucking in the bedcovers.

The Elephant & Castle

Dating from the seventeenth century, the Elephant & Castle is another of Amersham's reputedly haunted pubs. The curious title of the inn is believed to have two possible origins. It is thought to be either a corruption of 'Infanter of Castile', a title conferred on a seventeenth-century Spanish princess, or a derogatory soubriquet bestowed upon two ladies of considerable height, girth and weight who were part of King George I's entourage of family, friends, courtiers and hangers-on, keen on royally approved advancement when the Hanoverians arrived in England in 1714 and ascended the British throne. Whatever the origins of the name, the pub is home to a number of ghosts, one of whom takes a fancy to pinching barmaids' behinds whilst they are in the pub's cellar. An ex-landlady of the inn believed the saucy spook to be that of a previous publican who was female, and who took a shine to the pub's young women. The apparition of the bottom-pinching ghost was seen at

The Elephant & Castle pub in Amersham supposedly haunted by a bottom-pinching ghost.

the inn one Christmas in a flat above the bar by the landlady's son. The figure, dressed in black, glided across the room before vanishing through a wall. Although the ghost of the cheeky spectre has not been seen at the inn for some time, her presence is still felt.

Woodrow High House

Woodrow High House stands just over a mile outside the centre of Amersham on the A404 towards High Wycombe and Hazlemere. The building generally dates to the eighteenth century, though part of the structure incorporates the fabric of an earlier seventeenth-century house. Following the Parliamentarian's victory in the English Civil War, Lord Protector Oliver Cromwell, together with his wife and four daughters, lived at Woodrow. Some thirty-five years after the defeat of King Charles I, the house once again gave shelter to another rebel keen to see the end of the Stuart dynasty. On 6 July 1685, the Battle of Sedgemoor was fought between the forces of King James II and the rebel James Scott, 1st Duke of Monmouth. Following Monmouth's defeat, his supporters dispersed and fled for their lives. One of these, Sir Peter Bostock, made his way to Woodrow High House with his fiancée, Lady Helena Stanhope. Bostock was hidden in a grotto within the grounds. His hiding place was soon discovered, and he was arrested and ultimately executed for his part in the Monmouth Rebellion. Lady Helena Stanhope, unable to bear the loss of her fiancée, committed suicide by swallowing poison.

It is the ghost of Lady Stanhope, the green lady, which is said to haunt Woodrow High House. In 1946 the house was donated to the London Federation of Boys Clubs. When the building was being converted for use by the federation, one of a team of men working in the house woke up in the middle of the night and heard somebody moving around downstairs.

Fearing it might be a thief out to steal the valuable tools and materials lying around, he got up to investigate. Silently creeping down the stairs, he was startled to see a woman dressed in green walking slowly along the corridor. At first he took the figure for a real woman, but she ignored his calls as she walked across the hall and, to his horror, passed straight through the window, which had formerly been the front door of the

Woodrow High House near Amersham, where the ghost of Lady Helena Stanhope is said to walk.

house. Now, thoroughly disturbed, the workman saw the ghost glide across the grounds to vanish on the edge of the surrounding woods.

He raced back upstairs to the room where the workmates were sleeping. His abrupt, frantic arrival woke up his colleagues who demanded to know the reason for the midnight fuss. They thought he must have been dreaming, or was trying to play a joke on them. Next morning, however, the men were to learn of the tragedy of Lady Helena and the belief that it is her ghost that haunts the house. Despite the men's reservations about working in a haunted building it was decided there was little that could be done about the ghost, and the work proceeded, but without further incident.

The ghost of Lady Stanhope has also made her presence felt in other ways. John Fidgett, deputy director of the Residential and Training Centre for London Youth at Woodrow House, said:

We were rearranging some furniture in a room that has two huge portraits of Lady Stanhope and Sir Peter Bostock side-by-side. The builders removed the picture of Bostock and took it downstairs to the cellar. The next morning the portrait of Lady Stanhope had fallen off the wall and was face down on the floor, directly above the cellar. There was no sign of forced entry and the dust that had settled overnight had not been disturbed. It would take two strong men to have lifted that picture off the wall. It's really spooky and I won't allow the portraits to be separated from now on.

Perhaps the most astonishing observation of the green lady took place in January 1946. Terry Lawson, who was at the time the federation's secretary, arrived at the empty house to install electrical equipment. He was staying alone overnight, and before he retired to bed made a tour of the building to make sure all was secure. During the night, he was awoken by the sound of footsteps which came from the passageway outside his bedroom. Along with the footfalls was the sound of a swishing material which sounded on the floor of the corridor. Lawson quickly lit a candle and went out onto the darkened landing to investigate. But there was no one there. He returned to bed and was just falling asleep when he heard the downstairs grandfather clock chime three. Yet his watch told him it was just after midnight. As he listened he once again heard the sound of footsteps out in the passage. Again they were accompanied by a long swishing sound as if something was being dragged along the floor. The footsteps came up the stairs to his room, paused outside and then moved into an apartment known as the Cromwell Room.

Next morning, other people arrived at Woodrow and were excited to hear of Lawson's experiences of the previous night. The day was spent looking for secret passageways and panels they felt must exist in the house. That night, everyone retired to bed except one young lad who decided to undertake his own midnight ghost hunt. He silently left his room and crept down the corridor. On reaching the head of the stairs he heard footsteps approaching from behind. Thinking he had been discovered by a member of staff, he turned, and was astonished to see a spectral figure gliding towards him. He described the apparition as a woman dressed in green, with a look of urgency on her face. Ignoring the open-mouthed boy, she quickly passed him and descended the stairs. He followed her into the dining room just in time to see her pass through the centre window and out into the garden. With remarkable courage the young lad hastily pursued the phantom into the grounds and watched as she headed in the direction of the woods before she faded from view.

One might think that the young man's encounter with the ghost would be enough to unnerve him, but not so. He returned to the house and was stopped dead in his tracks as he watched the cellar door open of its own accord. Incredibly, there, once again, stood the woman in green. Now her expression was one of anger, and the boy noticed that she seemed to be weeping. She moved towards him, and as she glided past, the grandfather clock struck three. He followed her back up the stairs as she made her way towards the Cromwell Room. He watched as she entered and went over to a cupboard positioned in the wall. From it she took a bottle and began to drink deeply from its contents. Her face at once contorted into an expression of pain as she collapsed, seemingly in agony. The young man looked on in astonishment as the phantom woman writhed on the floor before vanishing.

Beaconsfield

Located some 4 miles to the south of Amersham, and 6 miles east of High Wycombe, Beaconsfield, like Amersham, has two centres. The old town is an attractive location containing a number of fine Georgian buildings and pubs. The wide high street is reminiscent of a town that was an important staging point on the coach route between London and Oxford. The new town to the north grew up around the railway line, and was at one time separated from old Beaconsfield by open countryside. The town is home to the world's oldest model village, and the Beaconsfield film studios. Many British comedy movies were produced at the studios, with the town's streets and roads being used as locations. The ghost stories which follow come from two distinctly different periods and buildings.

The Royal Standard of England Inn

The Royal Standard of England Inn on Brindle Lane, just west of Beaconsfield new town, is thought to be the oldest free house in England. It was originally called 'the Ship', and dates from 1213. In 1663 it became The Royal Standard of England in honour of the restored King Charles II, following the fall of Cromwell's commonwealth. The inn had offered supporters of the merry monarch's father, Charles I, a 'safe haven' during the English Civil War. With its connections to the Civil War it would seem appropriate that one of the ghosts said to haunt the pub is that of a phantom drummer boy. The sounds of a beating drum that can be heard in the car park are believed to be the ghost of a young drummer who served with the Royalists during the struggle between Roundheads and Cavaliers. Curiously, the pub was used as a mustering place for the Royalists. This would seem not only a little odd, but also foolhardy, given the fact that during the Civil War Beaconsfield supported Parliament.

High Wycombe, only 6 miles to the east, was also a Roundhead stronghold, as was Aylesbury to the north. Indeed, the Royal Standard could be said to have been situated deep within enemy territory. Even so, the pub had connections with Irish adventurers coming over to fight for the Stuart cause. In November 1642, they were part of a Cavalier army led

The oldest free house in England, the Royal Standard, is haunted by a phantom drummer boy.

by the dashing Prince Rupert who captured Brentford. The following day they were turned back at Turnham Green just outside London by an army raised from the Capitals trained bands. The pub was subsequently besieged by Parliamentarian forces, and the Royalist defenders suffered the wrath of the Roundheads, with a dozen Cavaliers having their heads raised up on pikes outside the door, including a twelve-year-old drummer boy.

Another ghost that is said to walk the pub is a shadowy male figure, which strides across the bar and then disappears in the wall next to an old fireplace in the candle room. It is thought the phantom is that of one of the executed Cavaliers. However, many believe the ghost to be a traveller accidentally killed by the notorious Earl of Barrymore, one of a titled family originating in Ireland in the thirteenth century. In 1788, Barrymore was one of a band of rouges known as the Four Horse Club. They were a group of wild, young regency bucks who indulged in drunken, raucous behaviour, and would bribe any coachman to give them the reins and drive at breakneck speed. One of their drunken escapades resulted in a traveller to the inn being crushed outside the pub by a speeding coach and four. The bloody corpse was brought into the bar and the landlord was paid to keep his mouth shut over the incident, and a figure has been haunting the area downstairs ever since.

The Chiltern Cinema

The Chiltern Cinema, situated on the high street of new Beaconsfield, was opened in 1927, and for many years the popular movies of the day played to full houses. After it had been owned by a number of different proprietors it was bought in 1960 by the local council so that it could be used as a theatre. With the rise and popularity of television in the '60s there began a thin time for cinema attendance, and the Chiltern was in danger of being closed down. However, under the inspired management of Walter Gay,

the cinema's fortunes revived and once again began to play to a packed auditorium.

In 1979, the year after Walter Gay died, paranormal incidents began to be reported at the Chiltern. The apparition of a thin, grey-haired man was seen walking in the aisle, which was identified as Walter Gay. His ghost was also observed standing on the stage. On one occasion, shortly before the cinema was about to close, a member of staff noticed a figure sitting in one of the stalls. Assuming the person must have fallen asleep, she went to inform the manager, but when they returned the figure had gone.

Poltergeist activity was also experienced at the cinema. The manageress at the time, Claire Matthews, who lived in a flat above the premises, reported many strange occurrences. Various things were moved, or even smashed, and doors were slammed shut when there was no one near them. At night she would often hear the toilet flush, and in the morning would find evidence of poltergeist activity in the bathroom.

Despite the spooky goings-on at the cinema, Claire was not in any way alarmed by the incidents. She did notice, however, that the phenomena became particularly active when any of her friends came to stay, as if it disapproved of their presence in the flat. The cinema, too, was a target for paranormal phenomena. Doors that

The old Chiltern Cinema in Beaconsfield, where the ghost of former manager, Walter Gay, has been seen.

had been closed at night were found to be wide open the next morning. During the showing of a film, the mechanically operated curtains closed by themselves and could not be opened, resulting in the audience having to be refunded.

Today, the Chiltern is no longer a cinema and, before being converted to a trendy restaurant, was a children's indoor adventure play park. It would seem that the exuberance and energy of the kids letting off steam as they played in the once haunted cinema has banished the ghostly activity, as there have been no further reports of paranormal phenomena, and the spectre of Walter Gay is no longer seen.

Chesham

Chesham, some 12 miles north-east of Wycombe, was built up around the twelfth-century church of St Mary, which is believed to have been built on a prehistoric holy site. The name of the town is thought to derive from the old English 'Caestaelesham', meaning 'the river meadow at the pile of stones'. There is evidence that the area was settled as early as the late Mesolithic period around 5000 BC. Today, the town is a mixture of old and new. British writer, presenter and wit, Stephen Fry spent part of his early childhood in Chesham attending the preparatory school. Lewis Carroll's celebrated *Alice in Wonderland* includes the character the Mad Hatter, which was said to have been based on Chesham resident, Roger Crab.

The hamlet of Pednor, on the outskirts of Chesham, is said to be haunted by a ghost. Within a week, but on two separate occasions, two motorcyclists travelling along the road encountered a figure in black which was sitting on a gate. As they approached the figure it suddenly jumped off the gate and into the path of the bike. The motorcyclists both reported that they struck the figure, but on investigation the person was nowhere to be seen and the road was deserted.

Another extraordinary ghost which is said to haunt the town was encountered by a motorist driving his van along a lane close to the railway station one night in December 2010. From a slip road, a tall man in brown emerged into the path of the van, and the driver immediately swerved to avoid him. But, incredibly, as the van proceeded along the road, the figure in brown began to run alongside until it quickened and moved ahead of the vehicle before vanishing.

Chesham is not, as one would expect, without its haunted houses. Yet those ghosts or spectres which desire to make their presence felt in their chosen abode can, as we have seen, be benevolent or otherwise. The following example demonstrates that in some cases ghosts can be downright nasty. The tenants of the property where the next incident took place have requested, not surprisingly, that the location be withheld.

Early in January 1994, a young family were allocated a three-bedroom council house in the centre of the town. After living in a cramped one-bedroom flat for eight years they were eager to do up their new home, and were soon busy painting and decorating and turning the small modern house into a comfortable family residence. However, despite the parents' enthusiasm for their new home, two of their children seemed to intensely dislike the house and could not settle there. The eldest boy, six-year-old Jamie, found it difficult to sleep and soon started to have nightmares, waking up screaming in the night.

Three weeks into their tenancy, Sandra, the wife, woke suddenly one night when she felt a heavy 'bump' against the side of the bed. Sitting up to see what had caused the noise she looked across the room and saw that the curtains were moving, as if a draught were playing against them, yet the window was shut and there was no breeze. The movement soon stopped and Sandra, even though puzzled by the incident, went back to sleep.

Next morning, however, she felt that there had been a change of atmosphere in the house. She couldn't put her finger on it, but everything seemed different and a sense of unease began to settle over her.

Over the following weeks, as she and her husband, Paul, continued with the decorating, they began to hear regular unexplained bumps and knocks sounding throughout the house. Jamie still seemed nervous, becoming very clingy and following his mother everywhere and not wanting to go to school.

Things soon took an alarming turn when the couple awoke one night to feel their bed shaking. Sandra also had the uncomfortable sensation of someone stroking her hair or touching her arm. The sense of unease now became almost unbearable for the couple, and both expected that something terrible was forthcoming. Their utmost concern was for their children and they considered leaving the house. Yet it had taken them nearly nine years on the housing list to get the family home they had always wanted; they were not going to risk returning to the cramped flat they had only recently left.

The couple soon discovered that the previous tenants had both been mediums and belonged to a local spiritualist church. Was it possible that they had, at some time during their occupancy, contacted some form of entity which, after they had left, remained in the house and now chose to harm and frighten the new tenants? It seemed that Sandra was the focus of whatever was causing the disturbances; she increasingly found herself unable to sleep and would lie awake until the small hours. One night, as her husband slept beside her, she looked across to the open bedroom door. Out on the darkened landing she became aware of two piecing pinpricks of light which grew in size and luminosity. Sandra stared intently at them until she realised that they were two red eyes looking at her from the darkness. Her screams woke Paul, but when she turned on the light the eyes vanished.

Such was Sandra and Paul's concern over what was happening that they decided to have the house blessed by a local rector. Yet this seemed to make things worse. One afternoon, when her mother and sister were visiting the house, Sandra went upstairs to the toilet with Jamie. On entering the bathroom, she was suddenly gripped by an overwhelming sense of evil. At once she became cold and terrified, and found it hard to breath. Her screams alerted her mother and sister, and both rushed from the living room to see Sandra, holding tightly onto Jamie, come tumbling down the stairs screaming, 'It's got me, it's got me!' Incredibly, her terrified pleas were uttered in the gruff voice of an old man. This was all too much for Sandra's mother and she at once hurried her daughter and the children out of the house and took them home with her.

It now seemed impossible that Sandra could return to the house and live there in peace. The local council were made aware of what the family had experienced, and alternative accommodation was provided for them. Is it possible that not only houses, but also people, can become haunted? Sandra's ordeal is not unique, as cases such as the Enfield and Pontefract poltergeist hauntings can testify. To date, Sandra has never again experienced, or been the victim of, paranormal phenomena, and the house the family had waited eight, patient years for has new tenants and is seemingly free of ghosts.

Great Missenden

Great Missenden lies at the head of the Misbourne Valley. The name is thought to derive from the old English words 'Mysse' and 'Denu', meaning 'the vale where the water plants grow'. By 1086 it was recorded in the Domesday Book as 'Missenden'. The village is overlooked by the medieval parish church of St Peter and St Paul. Its position away from today's centre suggests an earlier settlement round the church, with a move to its present location in the early Middle Ages. Missenden Abbey was founded in 1133

as an Augustinian monastery. It was abandoned following the Dissolution of the Monasteries and the remains were incorporated into a Georgian mansion, which is now a conference centre and college. The main street of the village is lined with many attractive half-timbered buildings dating from the sixteenth to the eighteenth centuries. Celebrated children's author Roald Dahl lived in Missenden from 1954 until his death in 1990. He was laid to rest in the village churchyard.

The Black Monks of Missenden

The dissolution of the monasteries by King Henry VIII between 1536 and 1541 was, ostensibly, a means by which the Tudor monarch could lay his hands on the considerable wealth and land that had been acquired over the centuries by the many religious orders throughout England. Missenden Abbey was no exception. The original endowment of the abbey included land at Great Missenden, with other parcels of land in the counties of Buckingham, Oxford and Huntingdon, as well as the churches of Great Missenden, Great Kimble, Chalfont St Peter, Weston Turville and its chapels in Caversfield and Shiplake in Oxfordshire

Over the years, the practice of providing spiritual guidance and succour to the local community had long been neglected by the monks, and stories of monastic impropriety, vice and neglect resulted in the

Great Missenden Abbey, now a training college, where the ghosts of a monk and phantom woman have been witnessed.

brothers ceasing to play a leading role in the religious life of the area. The monks of Missenden were, it seems, eager to indulge in worldly pleasures. Many of the town's inns were a frequent attraction to the clerics who had forsaken their clerical robes for more secular attire, and many were reported as stumbling out of ale houses, shouting, dressed in doublet and jerkin, and carrying swords.

The brothers' indulgences also extended to the nuns of a convent situated half a mile from the abbey, which, it is said, were connected by a secret tunnel allowing the monks to pass unnoticed when they sought the pleasure of the 'sisters of mercy'. In 1297, there seems to have been an attempt to tighten up discipline after one young novice was caught in a compromising situation with a nun from the convent. Fearing the consequences, it is believed that he cut his throat in a chamber by the minstrel's gallery overlooking the dining room. It is thought that it is his ghost that today haunts the conference centre and college that stand on the site of the former abbey. The ghostly cries of his desperate end have been heard echoing throughout the building, with staff working late at night hearing an eerie, wailing sound in the corridors.

It is thought that the ghost of the monk also haunts Little Abbey Hotel, once the site of the twelfth-century convent and which today is a private hospital. One day, a handyman carrying out repairs on the windows saw a figure in a brown hooded cloak coming up the stairs towards him. The brother of mercy had his hands together as if in prayer. Strangely, as the monk passed, the workman took him to be a real person and greeted the cleric with a cheery 'good morning'. After some time the monk had failed to reappear, and knowing that there was only a toilet on the top floor, the other rooms used by staff being locked, the workman went to see where he had got to, and if he had locked himself into one of the cubicles. As there was no other way downstairs, the figure in the brown cloak would have had to pass the handyman. But he found the toilet empty and all the other rooms locked and deserted.

The monk is also said to walk in the grounds of the abbey and the water meadows to the south. With downturned head and unhurried footsteps, he has been seen wandering across the grass at all hours of the day and night. Occasionally the apparition is observed heading east towards the church of Saint Peter and Saint Paul where the monks would sometimes preach.

The ghosts of phantom monks are not the only spectres reported at the abbey. Two students sat reading one day, near the staircase, when they were startled to see a figure floating down the stairs and out through the door. They described the apparition as an old woman in a crinoline dress. In 1972, another student reported seeing a similar figure near one of the ladies cloakrooms. She is described as grey, sometimes white, and on occasion has been dressed in black. The identity of the female ghost is unknown, yet it would appear that she is an unhappy spirit; on one occasion a vase was thrown down the stairs, and in the 1970s a heavy glass ashtray was found smashed in pieces in one the students bedrooms.

Another ghost said to haunt the abbey and the village is that of Hugh de Plesseter, Lord of Missenden, who died in 1292. He left instructions that he should be buried, seated on his horse, before the abbey's high altar. The monks did not take kindly to the unusual request, but they dared not refuse and the lord's wishes were carried out. Nonetheless, it would seem that de Plesseter's desire for a prominent last resting place did nothing to sooth his immortal soul as it is said that on stormy nights the fearsome ghost of the Lord of Missenden returns to ride, thundering on his war horse through the village.

On the other hand, the phantom rider might well be Sir John de Plessis, who, like Sir Hugh de Plesseter, also requested that he be buried by the high altar of the abbey, sitting upright on top of his favourite steed. The executors of his will made it so, yet once again it would appear that such a privileged burial chamber does not guarantee everlasting peace, as the ghost of Sir John has also been seen riding along the hills and through the village.

There seems to be some confusion as to which phantom horseman it is who gallops through Missenden at night. It could well be the spectre of the eccentric, nineteenth-century soldier, Captain Backhouse, who requested that he be buried standing upright, sword in hand, in the back garden of his house. Despite being granted his wishes, the ghost of Backhouse was reported to ride madly through the village. Permission was sought to re-inter him in Great Missenden churchyard in the hope that burial in consecrated ground might curtail the soldier's mad midnight dash. This was done and proved effective, as the good captains ghostly gallops ceased.

If that wasn't enough, a fourth spectral rider is said to ride through the village at night. It is thought to be an unknown female phantom rider who bestrides her horse carrying her

Great Missenden high street, haunted by no less than four phantom riders.

The George Inn on Great Missenden high street, the haunt of a spectral monk and a pipe-smoking ghost.

The Co-op supermarket (formerly Somerfields) near Great Missenden station, where the ghost of a middle-aged man was allegedly captured on video.

head in her lap. With the ghosts of Sir John, Sir Hugh, Captain Backhouse and the phantom woman all vying for prominence on their ghostly rides, one could forgive the residents of Missenden High Street for thinking that they live on the last furlong of a spectral racecourse.

Phantom horsemen and women aside, the village itself also contains a number of alleged haunted houses and phantoms. The George public house in the high street has been the site of reported poltergeist phenomena. The pub is also said to contain a haunted chair. The chair was regularly used by a local man who used to sit there, smoking his pipe. Following his death, anyone who sat on the chair reported the overwhelming aroma of tobacco.

It is outside the pub that the apparition of the phantom monk has

been seen. The George dates back to the thirteenth century, and it is thought that the inn was a favourite watering hole for those Missenden monks who preferred their worldly pleasures to religious piousness.

A similar encounter to that experienced by a window cleaner at Burghleighfield House at Loudwater, High Wycombe, took place at a property on Missenden High Street. In the 1970s, a glazier installing new windows in a seventeenth-century house saw a figure dressed in black enter the room on which he was working. What shocked the workman was that he knew without a doubt that the house was locked and empty at that time.

Our last haunting in Missenden demonstrates that ghosts are not only to be found in the town's ancient medieval buildings and centuries-old inns and houses. The Somerfield supermarket (todays Co-op store), adjacent to the railway terminus on station approach, was built in the 1970s. Since 1980 it has been the site of paranormal phenomena, and is reputed to be haunted by an apparition of an unknown man. Members of staff at the store have reported goods flying off the shelves and unseen hands tugging at the female workers' hair. The supermarket's interior doors are said to open and close on their own and many employees have experienced unexplainable drops in temperature whilst working in the building. The majority of strange incidents have been reported taking place early in the morning before the store is open to the public and when staff are on their own. Disembodied voices and shouting have been heard in the warehouse at the rear of the shop. When investigated, there is nothing to account for the sounds.

Incredibly, the phantom is said to have been captured on the store's CCTV. Each night, after the supermarket was closed and the staff had departed, the security cameras were left running, scanning the shop and offices. Examining the footage the next day, the manager was astounded to see that the cameras had recorded an indistinct shape moving through the store. Even though it was hard to clearly define, the figure most resembled the appearance of a middle-aged man who was seen to wander up and down the aisles before gradually disappearing. When word spread about the spook being caught on camera, the media flocked to Missenden in the hope of a genuine ghost story. However, the management of the supermarket, rather bizarrely, declined to release the video recording, citing safety grounds as a reason, adding that the position of the CCTV cameras would be revealed if the footage was viewed, thereby compromising the security of the store.

To date, the phantom caught on video has not put in another appearance at the superstore. That is not to say, however, that the Co-op is no longer haunted; as we have seen throughout this book, be they phantom coaches, women in black, unearthly vehicles, spectral horseman, or crying infants, we just never know when a ghost is going to show up.

FURTHER READING

Adams, P. and Brazil, E., *Extreme Hauntings: Britain's Most Terrifying Ghosts* (Stroud: The History Press, 2013)

Adams, P., Brazil, E. and Underwood, P., *Shadows in the Nave: A Guide to the Haunted Churches of England* (Stroud: The History Press, 2011)

Ashford, L.J., *The History of the Borough of High Wycombe: From its Origins to 1880* (London: Routledge and Keegan, 1960)

Hepple, Leslie W. and Doggett, Alison M., *The Chilterns* (Stroud: Phillimore & Co., 1994)

ABOUT THE AUTHOR

EDDIE Brazil was born in Dublin in 1956, and was later raised in London. His first encounter with the paranormal occurred at the age of ten when, at his family home in Stockwell, the sound of disembodied footsteps made him flee the house in terror. It was an experience which led to a lifelong fascination with the supernormal, in particular the haunting of Borley Rectory, about which he has co-authored a definitive study. He has also written for magazines and the media. Together with veteran British ghost-hunter Peter Underwood and paranormal historian Paul Adams, he has written *Shadows in the Nave: A Guide to the Haunted Churches of England* and *Extreme Hauntings: Britain's Most Terrifying Ghosts*. Aside from ghost hunting his other interests include photography, church architecture, exploring the sites of former battlefields, surreal art, the history of youth subculture, and the classic ghost stories of M.R. James. He is also a guitarist and composer, and in 1983 wrote the theme music to the British comedy movie, *Expresso Splasho*. He is currently working on a book of original photographic interpretations of the ghosts of M.R. James. Eddie has lived in High Wycombe since 1986 and at present lives with his wife and daughter in Hazlemere, Buckinghamshire.

Eddie Brazil. (Courtesy of Rebecca Brazil)

If you enjoyed this book, you may also be interested in …

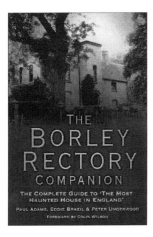

The Borley Rectory Companion
PAUL ADAMS, EDDIE BRAZIL & PETER UNDERWOOD

Borley Rectory, built in 1862, should have been an ordinary Victorian clergyman's house. However, just a year after its construction, unexplained footsteps were heard within the house, and until it burned down in 1939 numerous paranormal phenomena were observed. In 1929 the house was investigated by paranormal researcher Harry Price, and it was he who called it 'the most haunted house in England'. After his death in 1948, many claimed that Price's findings were not genuine, and ever since there has been a debate over what really went on. This book is a comprehensive guide to the history of the house and the ghostly (or not) goings-on there.

978 0 7509 5067 1

Extreme Hauntings:
Britain's Most Terrifying Ghosts
PAUL ADAMS & EDDIE BRAZIL

The most terrifying British ghosts are brought together in this unique and original compilation of spine-chilling true encounters both ancient and modern. Not for the faint of heart, this book contains over thirty compelling experiences, from the mysterious happenings at Hinton Ampner to the eerie Black Monk of Pontefract, the celebrated Enfield Poltergeist and the sinister power of the Hexham Heads.

978 0 7524 6535 7

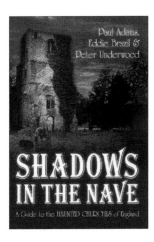

Shadows in the Nave:
A Guide to the Haunted Churches of England
PAUL ADAMS, EDDIE BRAZIL & PETER UNDERWOOD

The haunted history of England's churches and chapels is brought vividly to life in this comprehensive and beautifully illustrated modern guide. Here you will encounter the compelling world of the unseen linked with a thousand years of worship, including the Tudor phantom of Rycote, the lonely monk of Minsden Chapel and the black-magic ghosts of Clophill, to name but a few.

978 0 7524 5920 2

Visit our website and discover thousands of other History Press books.

www.thehistorypress.co.uk

18684147R00055

Printed in Great Britain
by Amazon